DANCE IN SC

DANCE IN SCHOOLS

by SUE LEESE and MOIRA PACKER

Heinemann Educational Books
London

Heinemann Educational Books Ltd
22 Bedford Square, London WC1B 3HH
LONDON EDINBURGH MELBOURNE AUCKLAND
HONG KONG SINGAPORE KUALA LUMPUR NEW DELHI
EXETER(NH) KINGSTON PORT OF SPAIN

© Sue Leese and Moira Packer 1980
First published 1980

British Library C.I.P. Data

Leese, Sue
   Dance in schools.
   1. Dancing – Study and teaching
   2. Dancing – Children's dances – Study and teaching
   I. Title II. Packer, Moira
   793.3'2'0712   GV1753.5

ISBN 0-435-80540-1

Printed and bound in Great Britain by
Biddles of Guildford

In memory of Chris Mattison

with thanks to Eric and all our friends

CONTENTS

1 Introduction and Aims
Introduction — 1
The aims of dance — 2

2 Dance in the School
How to start and develop dance — 4
Styles of dance — 5
Technique — 5
Dramatic dance — 5
Lyrical dance — 6
Folk dance — 6
Social dance — 6
Jazz dancing — 6
Stage dancing — 7
Tap dancing — 7
Religious or liturgical dance — 7

Starting a dance club — 8

3 Making a Dance
The body as a whole — 9
Body actions — 10
Parts of the body — 12
Body shapes — 15
Relationships — 17
Partner work — 17
Group work — 18
Technique — 19

Movement exercises — 23
Swinging actions — 23
Head — 26
Shoulders — 27
Arms — 29
Chest — 31
Spine — 33
Hips — 35
Legs and feet — 36
Trunk — 42
Complete actions — 44

Space
Personal and general space — 47
Levels — 47
Directions — 47
Peripheral and spoke-like movement — 48
Pattern — 48
48

Quality - how the body can move and express — 49
The four elements — 50
Combination of Efforts — 50

Stimuli
51
Stimuli through sound — 51
Visual stimuli — 52
Kinesthetic awareness — 52
Relationships as a stimulus — 53

4 The Preparation and Presentation of Dance

Preparation
54
Overall aims of dance — 54
The immediate and personal aims of the teacher — 54
The needs and ability of the children — 54
Selection of material — 54

Composition
55
The theme or topic — 55
Material for the 'motif' based on the stimuli — 55
Building of the motif — 55
Structure of the dance — 56
Composition of the lesson — 56
An example of a lesson — 57

Presentation
59
Setting the scene — 60
Teaching through doing — 60
Presentation of stimuli — 60
The teacher's role — 61

5 Practical Examples of Dance Topics 65
6 The Use of Music
Music as stimulus 72
Music as accompaniment 72
With technique 72
With a pianist 72
As a presence 73
Percussion 73

The choice of music 73
Composing to music 74
The technical problems of using music 74

7 Conclusion 76

Bibliography 77

1 INTRODUCTION AND AIMS

Introduction

This book is aimed at the teacher, or student teacher, of dance in the middle and secondary school – not necessarily only the specialist but also the teacher who shows interest and enthusiasm for movement; a long training in dance is not a prerequisite.

In the last thirty years since the inclusion of dance in the curriculm of some schools there have been only a few books written, the most authoritative of these being based on the findings of Rudolf Laban. His original ideas were taken, as were the ideas of Ling fifty years earlier, as being the ultimate in combining the aims of education or life in general with the aims of physical education in particular. Laban devised an analysis of movement which generally is thought to be the most related to educational needs. His initial disciples interpreted his ideas and translated them into a form of expressive dance which has become known by Laban's own name of Modern Educational Dance. Unfortunately in this transition his ideas became rather stylized and as such they have lost some of their original inspiration.

We take Laban's analysis of movement as a starting point but integrate it with the understanding of movement that is generally available to the student or teacher involved in this area today.

To the average student or teacher interested in dance today the only literature available, although excellent in interpreting and summarizing Laban's work, is far too concerned with the chemistry of dance. The language has become esoteric – whether it was used as a shorthand or with the intention of protecting its own discipline. Laban did produce a comprehensive analysis but his disciples in using this as their bible have tended to restrict rather than extend the use of his ideas. We are hoping to simplify and clarify some of the ideas put forward in previous works by updating them and looking at dance in relation to educational aims today.

Through dance we are trying to achieve a mastery of the body by understanding its possibilities as well as its limitations. The possibilities can be increased by enlarging the natural vocabulary of the children, both verbally and kinesthetically. The limitations are their own rather than those imposed by the teacher. Any that the teacher does impose should only be to aid the actual learning process. This seems to be much more related to Laban's original concepts.

We have tried to consider the recent developments in dance at all levels today. The emergence of the professional dancer through the modern dance companies has given validity to dance as an art form. Its popularity as entertainment, as a social skill and as a recreative process has widened the appeal of dance to the general public.

The aims of dance

In considering the aims of dance we should look at what 'dance' means to the average schoolchild, teacher or parent. The answers tend to be very varied, covering styles from classical ballet to disco dancing. Fortunately they are not as diverse as they might at first appear. They do after all have one thing in common – the body! The word dance is actually very difficult to define.

1 Dance originates from emotional impulse and improvisation. (Max V. Boehn (1925) *Der Tanz* Berlin)
2 Dance is used to reveal inner moods and emerges as a result of an impulse. ((1934) *Der Grosse Brockhaus* Leipzig)
3 Dance is the expression of joy. (B.H. Schurtz (1900) *Urgeschichte der Kultur* Leipzig)
4 Dance is defined as the spontaneous activity of the muscles under the influence of some strong emotion, such as social joy or religious exultation; definite combinations of graceful movements performed for the sake of the pleasure which the exercise affords the dancer or the spectator. Carefully-trained movements which are meant by the dancer vividly to represent the actions and passions of other people. In the highest sense it seems to be for prose-gesture what song is for the instinctive exclamation of feeling. (W.C. Smith, A.B. Filson Young (1910), *The Encyclopedia Britannica* vol. VII)

A set of rules separates one form of dance from another – where the body moves, what it moves and how it assembles the movements will identify its own particular style. Another common factor is the *expressive* quality of the movement which is inherent in all dance since dance is an expressive rather than a functional mode of movement. The way in which the body is used to express a feeling or action will therefore determine the type of dance to be performed.

When teaching dance to children we are hoping to achieve many different things. The main aim, apart from enjoyment, should be to attain bodily control or body management. An awareness of the body as a physical presence and as an instrument of communication is an essential part of a child's education. By emphasising the importance of the body to the child, a greater mastery of movement can be achieved. In terms of safety alone this is a vital asset.

Physical education, and in particular dance, enables the teacher to observe children closely and have a more personal relationship with them. This in turn affords the teacher greater insight into the children's behaviour, for example the way in which the children form groups and work together can be very informative.

Children, particularly those who have difficulty in verbal expression, benefit from dance in many ways. After all, why should children be deprived of understanding the language of non-verbal communication? It is our natural heritage and for many it is the most easily-acquired skill and children can be seriously deprived if it is not included in the curriculum. Also the observation of each other's movement often leads to a greater understanding and acceptance of one's own and other's limitations.

One of the most important aims of teaching dance in schools today is to provide recreational opportunity for everyone within the currriculum, and especially recreation in a non-competitive atmosphere in which each individual achieves his own success. This does not imply that 'anything goes', but that each child may find satisfaction in his own contribution. The teacher must be aware of this function of dance and should try not to create barriers for the less able children. At times this may seem impossible, but it is more possible in dance than in games or gymnastics.

Whilst performance is an important aspect of dance, dance should be acknowledged for its therapeutic value alone. There are few other areas of education which offer the possibility of expression without examination or consequence. For example, in painting, the results of creativity remain visible to the artist and the observer. In dance without an audience the feeling of *doing* is what gives the satisfaction and its transient nature does not allow for criticism or self-analysis at a later stage.

Today there is an ever-increasing responsibility placed on the teacher to help the child adjust to the many demands of society. Children can gain tremendous confidence by feeling adequate in the socially-accepted modes of behaviour of their contemporaries. The ability to dance leads to acceptance which can have far-reaching effects on the personality.

2 DANCE IN THE SCHOOL

How to start and develop dance

The inclusion of dance in the curriculum may have to be fought for or justified although dance as a recreation in itself should be justification enough. Add to this its artistic value, and it is difficult to understand why it is not compulsory for every child of school age. The past attitudes of society may force the teacher to give reasons for the inclusion of dance in the curriculum today. Children love to move, but at a very early age society compels them to be suspicious of expressing themselves. Thus, the teacher's hardest task is to present dance to children in a meaningful and enjoyable way.

This is the starting point from which the teacher must work. First, the idea of dance must be sold to the children and this requires a great deal of enthusiasm, dedication and perseverance on the part of the teacher. The next step is to help them acquire the movement vocabulary that will enable them to create their own dances, interpret music and express ideas. The pupils' limited movement ability and experience must be taken into consideration.

It is extremely important to find a common denominator which will not only enable the teacher to understand the children, but also result in enjoyable activities and gradually develop the pupils' confidence. Every pupil should be made to feel secure and be helped by being given a certain amount of material with which to work. Success, however small, is important and each individual's contribution adds to this.

Naturally the age of the child or student is vital in determining the starting point, although when introducing dance at any age the principles remain the same. The difference comes in how the child can cope with any new area.

A good teacher will be able to assess the needs of her pupils and work from there. Progress will be steady and productive. If the steps are made simple and the task and expectations are kept within reach, the less able and the more talented will both be challenged. Children must be stimulated and inspired. The opportunity to observe and to be observed should also be encouraged. In this way, children become more aware of simple experiences and begin to relate them in movement terms. The teacher has a mammoth task for not only should she have total conviction and involvement in her work, but she must show unending vitality and enthusiasm.

The use of demonstration plays an important role in presenting dance. Photographs, magazines and theatre trips can add to this. Although there is an improvement in the dance available to pupils, there is still very little to be seen in the general media. So, whenever the opportunity arises of visiting a performing dance company, it should be seized.

Styles of dance

Dance as education should be an all-embracing experience. Just as art is not limited to painting, children should be given the opportunity of seeing, if not doing, all the different aspects of dance. Over the years the type of dance taught in schools has tended to become very stylized in one way or another. Whilst this is good and even essential in order for the teacher to have some kind of framework of reference, it is equally limiting in other ways.

Some kinds of dance require specific expertise – and the teacher cannot necessarily be expected to have the depth of knowledge in all these areas. It may be possible to ask an expert to come into a school to give a workshop or to show films or take children to see these different types of dance.

Other styles of dance are usually well within the range of most teachers; even if they are not absolutely authentic they can still acquire the feeling or the steps as necessary to add them to the whole dance programme. A brief explanation of a selection of these styles follows.

Technique

Various styles of technique should be experienced and they are all slightly different. Whenever possible children should be exposed to company or group workshops on technique and shown the differences and similarities.

The technique can and does in many cases dictate the style of dance as it trains the body in a particular way to achieve particular movements. To limit children to one technique can be good in that the security they feel can allow them to be more creative. On the other hand it may limit a style creatively as the body only learns one way of dancing.

Dramatic dance

This is probably the most commonly-used style. It usually involves a story, with full use of effort particularly and actions, whether the story-line is translated literally with characters or more abstractly, e.g. comic dances.

Lyrical dance

Another commonly-used style which places a greater emphasis on the spatial aspects and qualities. The pattern and the shape of the dance become the most important part. Very often a combination of the two is used with more experienced dancers to give maximum creative opportunity.

Folk dance

Many teachers are already familiar with folk dances of one kind or another. There are many ways they can be used in the school situation: to learn about other countries, to teach rhythm and coordination, to help achieve a communal class spirit.

New folk dances often look, and sometimes are, complicated to learn. It is very important and vital for the less experienced teacher to see them actually being danced rather than to read them step by step from a book in order to obtain the correct phrasing and character of the dance. There are many societies which would be willing to help by sending instructions or allowing teachers to join their groups.

Social dance

This is an area of dance rather shunned by some teachers. Nowadays, when the pressure is on children to conform, especially in public, it is very important to give them the opportunity to feel confident by teaching them basic steps and dances that would be helpful to them socially.

Ballroom dancing, whilst still important to a limited extent, has been more recently replaced by disco dancing. Disco dancing for many may still be a rather grey area but it is increasingly becoming a very definite art and style of dancing in its own right.

It is basically a combination of steps and movements put together in a way appropriate to the rhythm of the music of the time. Jive or the 'hustle' require as much teaching as the samba or the cha-cha and although the steps may be identical the music is certainly different.

Jazz dancing

Jazz dancing originated in the USA as a social dance and developed just as folk or ballroom dancing developed in England as part of the dance programme in schools.

Again it consists basically of a similar use of steps with and without syncopation but clearly defined by the demands of the music – this time jazz with its numerous time changes and intrigues.

It is another possibility to be added to the children's experience without a tremendous knowledge of the more developed step patterns and progressions.

Stage dancing

This particular style of dance has for a long time been considered the poor relation of other forms of dance. But in recent years the stage has produced some of the very best creative dance, with a big breakthrough coming in *West Side Story*.

At one time, when it was a decoration purely and simply, the value was limited. Now dancing on stage or film draws from many varied styles and often employs top choreographers of classical or modern ballet to help to add meaning and importance.

The value of this type of dance in school lies not only in the child's development within dance but also in the increased enjoyment in performance. School plays through to complete dance productions are important opportunities to share dance, and the 'communicating of movement as an art form cannot be achieved without the opportunity to dance before an audience.

Tap dancing

Tap is a branch of stage dancing which requires more specific skill but can be fun to do even in a limited way. If a dance club is run in the school then possibly an expert could be asked in to teach the rudiments.

Religious or liturgical dance

The opportunity can normally be found in a school to dance or perform dance as a form of worship or as an expression of religious feeling or belief or story. Most religions have a very long history of dance and lend themselves well to interpretation or expression through movement.

All the previous styles of dance can be put to very good use; lyrical dance for worshipping, dramatic for the stories or dramas, social, folk and stage, jazz dancing also all have their place in different ways. The subject has to be considered carefully and people's feelings respected. Usually, when done with the right motivation and appropriately executed even the fiercest of critics will be impressed.

Collaboration with different departments within the school is often very helpful here, as it is with every aspect of education.

Starting a dance club

Once dance has its place on the curriculum, the demand for more and more will only be satisfied by the formation of a club outside school time. Here children may mix with different classes, ages and sexes if this does not already happen in the class situation. It is an ideal opportunity to spend longer on techniques and to experiment with various styles as well as work towards the performing aspect.

Enjoyment again is the key factor, especially if trying to encourage membership. Working towards a production is also a very important experience for children, and in the less formal atmosphere of a club tremendous fun can be had by all. Children who wish to work in other ways with lighting or music or costume can benefit too from taking part in this kind of activity.

If it is difficult, or even impossible, to include dance in the school curriculum, a dance club is an excellent introduction for the children. One advantage might be that it could be a mixed club, which might help dispel the myth that dance is only suitable for girls. This may mean a more thoughtful approach is needed by the teacher as boys need to be convinced of the value of dance in society today.

3 MAKING A DANCE

Unlike a machine that can be switched on and off and programmed to do specific activities, the body is capable of performing many different actions. Its ability to explore all kinds of movements and emotions gives the body a versatility which is unique.

The basic movements of the body are, in everyday life, usually confined to extension, contraction and twisting of the whole or isolated parts. In dance, combinations of these together or against one another produce different relationships and convey the desired expression.

The fact that the body may be moving or still, and can use continuous movement or go and stop to produce a rather jerky flow all within the space of a few minutes enables tremendous variety to be achieved. More details about the change in speed and flow will be found later in descriptions of the control of the quality of movement. For the moment we are primarily concerned with how the body can move, the actions it can make and the implication of these actions.

Familiarity with the potential of the body in general and in particular is the most vital factor in dance. The different ways the body can move form the basis for the material, together with what is felt by the dancer and what can be conveyed to the audience.

To look in more detail at the possibilities of feeling and expression we must examine all the different aspects of movement.

The body as a whole

From the time a child is born the body gradually becomes stronger and the movements become more finely controlled. Initially the body moves as a whole, larger or total movements being easier to execute than smaller isolated ones.

To encourage children to use the body as a complete unit can be an exhilarating experience. Many ideas spring to mind when considering how to introduce this to a child. Two simple ways are first, to try to achieve complete extension throughout the body from fingers and toes right to the top of the head, and second, complete relaxation. Gradually other simple movements such as stretching, curling, jumping, bouncing, lifting and lowering can be introduced.

These different activities can be categorized into the basic body actions. In order for the teacher to understand the possibilities and show the children how they can move and how they can use such movement to express or convey ideas there follows a more detailed explanation.

Body actions

The actions that the whole body can do are discovered at a very early age. When dance is the objective the actions have to be re-established with greater clarity, and more variation can then be added.

The body can travel, jump, fall, turn and move without any specific action (normally called gesture).

Travelling

Travelling, although a very natural activity for any human being, when used in dance needs careful selection and control. There are many ways of travelling which include various parts of the body taking the weight, and transporting someone from one place to another. The feet can be used to step, producing walking or running or combinations of the two. Hopping and jumping are other ways of travelling on the feet. The step-like actions can be done with hands and feet producing handstands and cartwheels, or with different parts of the body taking the weight one after the other, for example, elbows, knees, shoulders placed on the floor successively. Jumping and hopping can be done from feet to hands — this would be a pounce. All parts of the body can move along the floor with sliding, rocking or rolling actions. The relationship of the body to the floor is important in adding variety to travel. For example, the body can be the right way up, upside down, back to, or side to the floor.

Lifting and carrying when children are working together in pairs or any size group may be done very sucessfully. Practice in bearing weight is important here – how to use the legs and back to prevent injury when taking someone's weight must be taught.

The expressive use of travelling

Weight transference, which is a major part of travelling, is one of the fundamentals of any expression. If movements are not well joined the meaning is totally lost. As in speaking, if the words do not join and flow easily it is hard to follow the train of thought.

Travelling in its own right is expressive of many things. It could show fear in retreating or joy in greeting, to give two obvious extremes.

Jumping and falling

Jumping to children is as natural as running and immediately shows great expression. In dance it can be executed in many different ways. The feet can be used to push off from and land on, together or separately. The choice will depend on the quality of jump required, whether it is symmetrical or asymmetrical, strong or light, small or large, or done with extension or contraction.

Combinations of travelling, turning and gesturing are also possible with jumping. Children need time to experiment with all these variations, as well with assisted jumps, where one or more than one child aids the other to achieve greater height either by lifting or by becoming a raised platform from which the child can take off.

A natural progression from jumping and landing is sinking and falling. Falling is equally expressive and just as there are correct ways to jump and control the body, so are there correct ways to fall. Control of the body in the air require practice in the right amount of tension, the appropriate approach and preparation of the position for take off and landing. To control the body in falling requires correct turning of the body and ordering of the parts to take the weight onto the floor.

The expressive use of jumping and falling

Jumping can express joy and happiness or fright. It can symbolize sheer strength and dominance or freedom from the bonds of gravity. Falling when used in dance can indicate weakness and defeat or depression at one extreme or strength and security in the closeness of the ground at the other.

Turning

To rotate around one's axis is to turn. It may be done by simply turning on one's feet or by moving different parts of the body to take the weight, for example, spinning and rolling. A turn can be a complete revolution, a fraction of a revolution, or several revolutions. A turn can be one in which the body opens out or closes in on itself or one in which the body changes its level. Slow turns, quick turns, symmetrical and asymmetrical turns are all possible. Combined with travelling and jumping they form the basis of all dance movement.

The expressive use of turning

A turn is very much a change of mind or rejection, a movement of turmoil or searching. When done in relation to another person or an object it makes a very strong statement.

Gesture

Gestures are often described as being the movements that change a functional movement into an expressive one. In some ways in using the previous actions expressively a gesture is being made. However, there is a more specific definition of gesture for the purposes of the student or teacher of dance. It is usually taken to mean a movement which does not involve the body in travelling, jumping or turning, although it is very often added to them, a gesture may be done without them. The whole body can gesture by using extension and contraction or opening and closing. Parts of the body may gesture independently in the same manner or by being lifted and lowered, turned and twisted, moved or held still. In this way dances can be done with just the hands or with different combinations of body parts. Generally it is used in conjunction with the other activities or interjected with other actions.

The expressive use of gesture

It is practically impossible to do a movement which can be described as a gesture without being expressive in some way, just as it is impossible to do any action without showing some expression of individuality. Because a gesture is often not a functional movement, the expression is highlighted. For example, waving the hand in greeting or parting, smiling, nodding or shaking the head are all gestures that are practically universal. Desmond Morris in his book *Man Watching* uses the word gesture for just such movements.

Much of the relevant use of gesture in dance can be taken from everyday actions although it can be transferred to other parts of the body and increased or diminished in size or weight to add to the variety of expression.

Parts of the body

The basic body actions may be done in many different ways and generally they involve the whole body. Naturally it would be impossible for a dancer to use the whole body throughout the dance. It would be both monotonous and extremely tiring for the dancer. Introducing the isolated use of different parts of the body must be the next stage of teaching dance. Every body part can be used separately; for example, the head alone may be twisted, turned and lifted up and down. Focus plays a vital part in dance and children must learn early the importance of the head.

Hands and feet can be experimented with to produce many different effects. Flexing the feet may lead to grotesque or comical movements as can the use of knees and elbows. The teacher therefore must present all the possibilities to the children but should also limit the actions to begin with otherwise they will become confused. Once emphasis has been laid on body parts, the natural progression is to take specific parts and begin reaching with them. Again, the variations are endless. For example, take the hand and consider all the different surfaces: the palm, the back, the fingertips or the side of the hand can each initiate a movement. The other more unusual areas such as the hips may be restricted in isolated use until the children learn more about rotation but they must not be overlooked. It is at this stage that the trunk area should be emphasized and the children be made aware of the individual muscles, stomach, back, neck, right and left sides, the chest and the shoulders. A dancer who does not open the chest can never produce a feeling of lightness or elevation. This should be stressed during all dance and can be worked on before a lesson begins. The hips and waist initiate any movement going through the centre of the body and without this vital link, dance lacks the feeling of sensitivity and completeness.

Symmetry and asymmetry

Both these movements are fundamentally simple for children to achieve and remember. Symmetry is when both sides of the body are doing the same movement and creating a strong secure and balanced feeling. Asymmetry is when there is more emphasis on one side of the body, leading to an unstable or more mobile sensation. The latter will mean the movements are fairly rapid and free moving whereas the former are more restricted in flow. It is interesting to see children put the two types of movement together and to see what kind of qualities emerge.

All the body actions can be done using both symmetry and asymmetry; for example in jumping the two-footed take off and landing will produce symmetrical movement whereas the one-footed take off will produce asymmetrical movement. Turning always has to be initiated asymmetrically but can become symmetrical in quality.

The expressive use of symmetry and asymmetry

Symmetry expresses balance, strength, control in many different ways. The different body shapes – pin or arrow-like, wall-shape and curled-up-ball shape – are all very powerful and expressive. Machine-like movement is generally best expressed by symmetry as the movement tends to be go-stop without special emphasis on travel. The vertical and horizontal lines show both aspiration and tranquillity.

Asymmetry expresses exactly the opposite, the offbalance lending itself more to travelling, twisting and turning. This can show confusion and indecision and complication expressing anguish, fear and uncertainty. The stress of the diagonal gives labile movement expressing the freedom vital in dances based on relationships and communication.

Simultaneous and successive movement

There are two ways in which movement can flow through the body. The first is simultaneous flow where different parts or the whole body move as a complete unit. Successive movement occurs when the flow spreads from one part to the next producing rippling or undulating movement. The difference in the flow in both types of movement produces very clearly opposing qualities that are difficult to separate and therefore often hard to understand. Children must be able to use both types of movement to increase their vocabulary. It is helpful for the teacher to note any preference in order that the children can be helped to develop the alternative. This applies to all preferred movement. The vocabulary can only be increased if the full range of possibilities is taken into consideration.

Simultaneous movement is often associated with symmetry as it produces a go-stop quality when one part of the body moves and stops before the next movement occurs. Examples of this can be seen in hopping, clapping and stamping.

Successive movement spreads more gradually, producing stretching, writhing, and lends itself more to asymmetry and so to travelling and reaching out.

The expressive use of simultaneous and successive movement

Because of the links with symmetry and asymmetry many of the expressive possibilities are the same. Simultaneous movement tends to stress the rhythmic quality and through clarity can produce confidence and decisiveness. This could just as easily express disunity, grotesqueness or show nervous tension.

Successive movement is generally more complicated and can be used to express a very wide variety of ideas. It can give a very lyrical and flowing feel to a dance if used with light quality. If used with strength, writhing, wriggling, twisted and tormented feelings emerge.

Extension and contraction

Extension and contraction of the body occur continually. Extension of the muscles or stretching can be a partial or whole-body movement. Yawning is a good example. Contraction of the muscles can be clearly seen in grasping. In dance they become exaggerated and extension is increased to produce an extreme feeling of stretch with strength or lightness. Contraction when initiated from the centre of the body can be likened to a concertina or squeezing action. This not only produces the opposite effect of extension but also increases the participation of the whole body which children find difficult.

The expressive use of extension and contraction

Extension and contraction are vital in expression. The energy required in achieving both extremes adds significantly to the feeling conveyed. Extension can be closely linked with communicating, and is often useful in expressing joy or confidence. Contraction, on the other hand, can convey insecurity, fear, tension, pent-up power or even solitude.

There is aesthetic satisfaction in seeing a body in complete extension or contraction in a purely abstract way. There is nothing less satisfying than seeing half-hearted physical commitment unless a state of relaxation, heaviness or lack of tension is what is required.

Body shapes

The body can make an infinite number of shapes on its own and in relation to others. These can be categorized into four basic shapes in order to simplify the teaching process.

The wall shape
This can be described as a flat, open, two-dimensional symmetrical shape that achieves a strong barricade or blocking effect. It may be made in many different ways: vertically, horizontally, or tilted, e.g. cartwheel. As an expression it tends to be powerful and barrier-like.

The pin or arrow shape
A one-dimensional shape, narrow, pin-like, achieved vertically or horizontally, producing a penetrating, splitting quality. This shape expresses strength in a different way, being more actively aggressive, more of a muscle than a wall in character.

The ball shape
A three-dimensional shape, small and curled, often close to the floor. The closed quality usually implies a shrinking away from and a defensive attitude.

In expression it is a vital contrast to the pin and wall shapes and with changing degrees of contraction can communicate a variety of meanings.

The twisted or screw-like shape
Another three-dimensional shape initiated by a twist in the trunk area. This produces asymmetric body shapes of endless animation. As with asymmetry in general expression it is usually related to anguish or conflict as one part moves against another, e.g. the body twisting against the feet planted in one direction.

Wall   **Pin**   **Ball**   **Screw**

Relationships

An individual moving in space has a relationship with his surroundings either consciously or unconsciously. If the awareness of this state can be increased then advantage can be taken of situations that may add to communication.

The dancer's relation to the space will be considered in more detail under the section on space, but the size and shape of the room or area in which the dance is taking place can have very significant effects on the movement. A small, poorly-lit area is not conducive to bold, expansive movements; a wide-open space would encourage free-flowing and more abandoned movement.

Relationships to the floor, the walls, an object or another person can be classified in a similar way. Also a dancer can be close to or far away from the object, facing it, back to it and sideways on.

An individual may also relate one body part to another in many different ways, for example, an elbow to a knee or a hand to a foot.

Something that a dancer may learn from an actor is the relationship to and with the audience. The distance from them, the interplay with them and the amount or neglect of eye-contact are all very interesting areas and worthy of consideration.

Partner work

When dancing with another person there are many varied opportunities for expression. One person can dance with or against a partner to produce reinforcement of a statement or an antagonistic, fight-like situation. Even in dancing with a partner there are so many possibilities it would be difficult to list them all. Identical movement can add weight to a statement; this can be done in varying relationships to the partner, for example, side by side, back to back, facing etc. Facing one's partner could also produce mirroring which can be quite a challenge for children's

Mirroring

observation and often lends itself to humorous movement. Shadowing is an offshoot of identical work but is often done so that an echo or shadow is achieved and the original movement is changed in some way, either in forcefulness – which would diminish – as in echoing, or with shadowing in ways which could lengthen or shorten. All these can be done with identical timing or they could be worked in canon with syncopation. One partner can always be completely still whilst the other moves, which produces an action-reaction situation, or a question followed by an answer.

The use of the space is very helpful in partner work. Once any distance comes between a duo then meeting and parting becomes more significant.

Contrasting

Partners can, of course, be contrasting or opposite in their movement. For example, one could extend when the other contracts. This could sometimes lead to a fighting situation. A more aggressive dance can be built up from action-reaction or contrast in body shapes, usually completely without contact but using the quality of the movement and the choice of actions to help convey the meaning.

Contact ranging from touch to support and balance is another important dimension of partner work. Work on balance and counterbalance can be done very simply and effectively without tremendous skill. Once lifts and supports are tackled more knowledge is required to avoid unnecessary strains. But again, if approached in a sensible way, this may develop into a significant area of partner work.

Group work

When attempting work in groups of three or more the range of possibilities is obviously increased but basically the alternatives are the same as in partner work. As the size of the group increases the possibilities increase and so the more difficult it becomes. For this reason large-group work, unless very carefully structured by the teacher, should not be attempted too early.

Circular group for motion

Some simple large-group shapes or patterns may be experimented with and even action and reaction between two groups, as between two people, could be a good lead-in to working with greater numbers. Also the use of a common group-focus is a good initial way of working in groups; the movements may be varied and the focus is the factor that binds them together.

Use of levels

Technique

Technique is rarely mentioned in detail or even at all in many dance books, but it is extremely important that every child has a knowledge of his body and is made aware of its capabilities and limitations. Margaret H. Doubler says, 'Technique transforms experience into the forms of its expression'.

Exercise is a natural requirement of the human body which needs almost continual movement. Even when sleeping the body changes position several times during the night. Take, for example, how we feel during a long car journey having sat in the same position for a number of hours. Our natural reaction is to get out of the car at some stage to take a walk and stretch our legs. In this way, much of the tension from driving is eased and the concentration needed regained.

Because of the nature of many desk jobs today there has been a great demand for 'keep-fit' and yoga classes. Those who attend these voluntary classes benefit not only physically but mentally. Instead of anticipating exhaustion at the end of a session, many people are invigorated and feel less tired. Although it may be an effort to attend these classes after a hard day's work, the rewards afterwards repay the time spent. By relieving tension and revitalizing the body, we not only look and feel better but our bodies will function better.

Many back complaints are caused by back muscles weak from under-use and incorrect posture. In schools we can deal with these problems at an early age and by introducing dance into the curriculum, children will become more aware of their bodies. It is here that we can begin to correct unfortunate habits such as slouching and shuffling. We are too ready to accept our faults and not too eager to attempt to correct them. None of us is perfect, but we can still help ourselves if we realize we have a problem in the first place. This is not for one minute a suggestion that we should inspect every child and tell him exactly what is wrong with his body or we may have more serious emotional problems to deal with, but it is a teacher's trained eye that can see the round-shoulders or the sagging tummies and give appropriate technique classes to correct these.

Our first aim is to *stretch* the body gently, particularly the ligaments, and therefore make us more mobile. *Gently* must be stressed otherwise we may find that doing too much vigorous exercise too quickly, especially for those not used to it, will result in extreme stiffness of the muscles and joints and often injuries such as pulled muscles may occur. Our second aim is to *strengthen* the body, which does not mean building it up to be 'muscle taut', but merely to prepare the body for greater feats in the exciting work ahead. The more we understand our bodies, the more we can produce by building up our vocabulary of movement. Closely united with our first two aims comes a third one – that of coordination. Without strengthening and stretching our bodies we cannot hope to gain the control essential for good coordination. We should learn to control our bodies and not vice versa. The human body requires proper use to function efficiently. It is very different from a machine that wears out with use; we must learn to respect it and exercise over and above the normal demands of daily living in order to maintain its efficiency. The resultant appearance and feeling are added benefits that cannot be overlooked. We can compare our joints to hinges; they must be 'oiled' with regular exercise otherwise they become less mobile and consequently less effective.

It is here that we should look at the aesthetics of the body – an indispensable element to every art form or sport, be it ballet, golf or modelling. One could not hope to become a good golfer without learning the correct stance or swinging action of the club. Likewise a ballet dancer could not hope to achieve a high standard without learning the correct carriage and posture of the body, or the sensitivity and dedication which is vital to the absolute success of any activity.

Technique is not therefore purely a series of mechanical drills but should be taught and expressed with sensitivity. Here dancers form the basis of their training; not only are skills learnt but the whole process of mental as well as physical activity must be combined to enable the dancer to express the aesthetic quality which is vital to dance, particularly at performance level. The ability to communicate is in us all and dance gives us a sense of purpose and a totality of mind, body and spirit.

There are several 'styles' of technique based on the principles of dancers such as Laban, Graham, Cunningham or Duncan, but it is important that the teacher does not necessarily slavishly follow one particular 'style' but decides what she believes in. The teacher should aim at instructing pupils to dance the way they want to and guide them in the right direction.

When teaching technique, it is usual to begin with a whole-body action such as a series of swinging movements, in order to loosen the muscles and joints. This is a vital activity before going on to more strenuous technique work.

In the following section are a series of possible movements which aim to strengthen, stretch and coordinate the body, making it more mobile. They are meant as an introduction and guide to the teacher and are by no means the only activities available.

Each of us will teach differently, and once more experience is gained we can build up our technique vocabulary, and once we realize the needs of our class we can deal with them accordingly. However, to begin with, it is advisable to start with a swinging activity and then work from the head to the feet or vice versa. We should begin on the floor and gradually work up to standing and jumping by which time the body will be well prepared.

It must be emphasized that it is not good to rush technique. It is far better to achieve the correct positions slowly than the wrong ones quickly! *Never* push a class beyond its own capabilities. *Stress* the need for 'feeling' the movement, whether it is opening, closing, extending, elevating or otherwise. See that the head is in the correct position as this will help accomplish the quality and perfection of the complete movement.

Movement exercises

Swinging actions

A

1
Standing tall with arms above head. Shoulders relaxed.

2
Swing arms down. Bend knees.

3
Bounce on heels swinging arms back fingertips brushing the floor

4
Behind.

5
Swing arms forward

6
Through

7
To standing again.

Repeat

Teaching points

This is excellent for loosening the body. Let the head go with the movement. Keep heels on the floor throughout. Bounce down in 3, lifting arms back in 4, bouncing on heels again when swinging through to 5. This should be done fairly quickly.

B

1 Stand with arms above head right foot in front of left foot about 30 cm apart. Weight evenly placed in centre.

2 Keep right leg straight. Swing arms down towards floor

3 Backwards brushing fingers along the floor

4 Bouncing on heels keeping heels flat on the floor

5 Lift arms back.

6 Bounce on heels again lifting arms forwards brushing back of fingers along the floor

7 Lifting up

8 Until straight.   Repeat

Teaching points

Check that weight is evenly distributed for 1. Take weight onto back foot when swinging downwards, bending the back leg. Keep heels on the floor throughout.

C

1 Standing, arms stretched out at shoulder level legs apart, feet slightly out-turned.

2 Keep heels on the floor. Drop head and arms down towards floor – sweeping action. Bend knees

3 Bring arms towards one another fingers brushing the floor

4 Cross arms

5 As far as possible bouncing action down and up.

6 Uncross arms bouncing down. Back of fingers brushing floor

7 Towards

8 Original

9 Starting position.   Repeat

Teaching points

Heels must be kept on the floor throughout. Drop head with the action, bouncing down crossing arms. Knees should move out over big toes.

Head

A

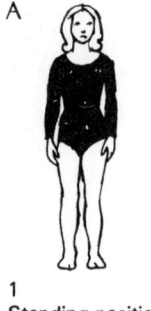   

1
Standing position
relax shoulders

2
Slowly bend
head to right

3
Bring head back
to centre

4
Slowly bend
head to left.

Repeat 1 to 4 five times

Teaching points

Emphasize the relaxed position in 1, particularly in the shoulders. The head should be moved slowly. This activity will relieve tension in the neck.

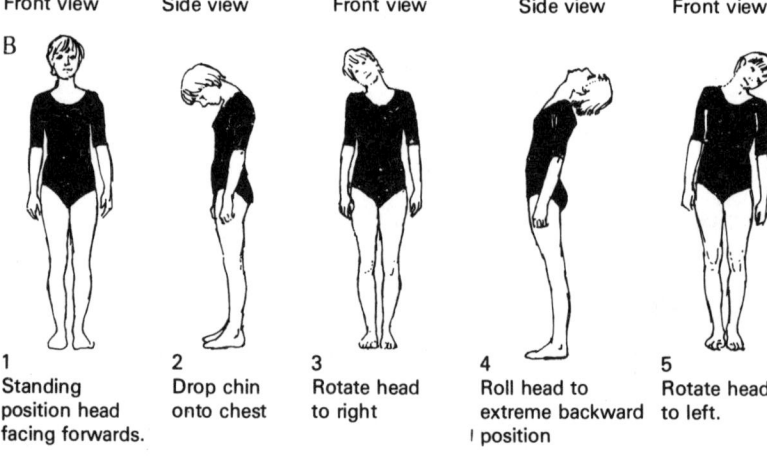

Front view | Side view | Front view | Side view | Front view

B

1
Standing position head facing forwards.

2
Drop chin onto chest

3
Rotate head to right

4
Roll head to extreme backward position

5
Rotate head to left.

Repeat 1 to 5 anti-clockwise, then five times clockwise, five anti-clockwise

Teaching points

Relaxed shoulders are again essential. Stop momentarily in each position.

Shoulders

A

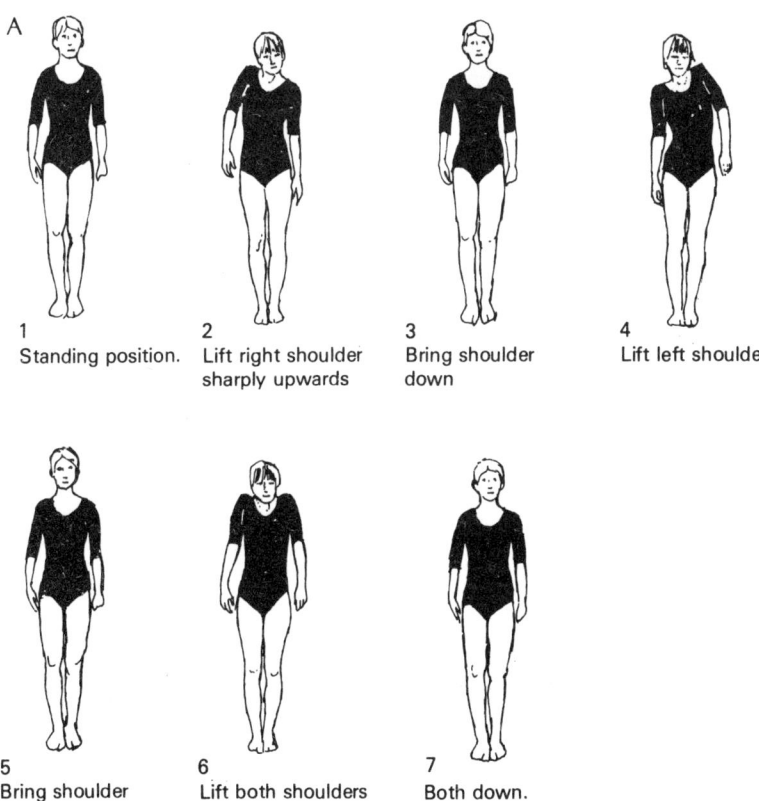

1 Standing position.
2 Lift right shoulder sharply upwards
3 Bring shoulder down
4 Lift left shoulder
5 Bring shoulder down.
6 Lift both shoulders up.
7 Both down.

Repeat 1 to 7 five times.

Teaching points

This is a simple method of helping children to relax their shoulders. Be sure that when one shoulder is raised the other is relaxed.

B

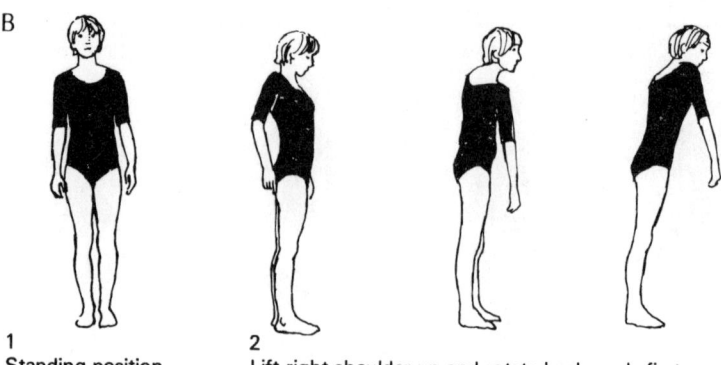

1
Standing position.

2
Lift right shoulder up and rotate backwards first.

Repeat five times right side. Repeat five times on left. Then five times together.

Teaching points

These should be done slowly and with as much rotation as each individual is capable of achieving. This is excellent for helping children achieve more mobility in their shoulder joints.

C

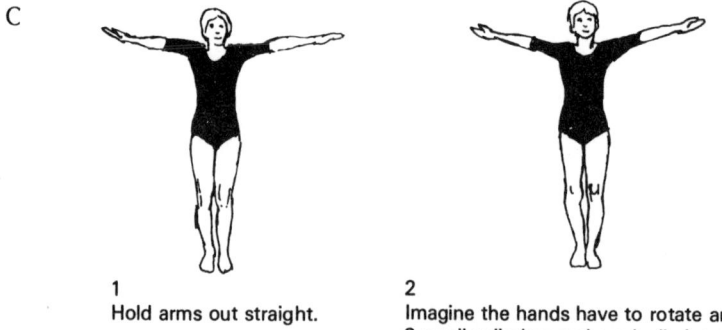

1
Hold arms out straight.

2
Imagine the hands have to rotate around 2 small cylinders and gradually introduce the shoulders so that they also rotate forwards and backwards.
Repeat ten times.

Teaching points

Ensure that shoulders do not rise. This will strengthen the arm muscles and give an 'open' feeling in the chest. Make sure that the back is very straight before beginning.

Take this activity even further to develop an opening and closing movement.

D

1
Palms uppermost arms straight.

Repeat three times

2
Rotate shoulders forward contracting in centre. Bend knees slightly, palms face back of room.

3
Rotate back to 1 lifting centre until back is straight again and palms uppermost.

Teaching points

Contract in the centre for 2, ensuring that all the movements are *slow*.

Arms

A

 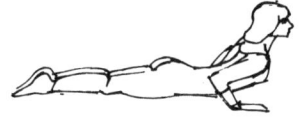

1
Lie down on the floor place hands beneath shoulders fingers pointing towards one another.

2
Slowly tilt head back and lift trunk by pushing down on hands.

3
Arch spine straighten arms head back.

4
Return to first position.

Teaching points

Not only will this strengthen arms but it will also make the spine more flexible. It will help to count 10 beats to lift up to 3, hold for 10, and lower to 4 for another 10. This will help children become more aware of rhythm and coordination.

B

1 Standing relaxed.

2 Lift arms slowly to shoulder height in front.

3 Take arms out to side shoulder height

4 Lift arms up to head also keep shoulders relaxed.

5 Bring arms down to side.

Repeat three times

C

1 Relax.

2 Lift spine off floor keeping shoulders and posterior on the floor. Chin should come onto chest.

3 Relax.

Teaching points

This is an easier position to achieve and isolates the back muscles. Try to imagine that a 'hole' is being made when the back is arched in 2 and get children to do this in pairs and see if they can 'look' through the 'hole'.

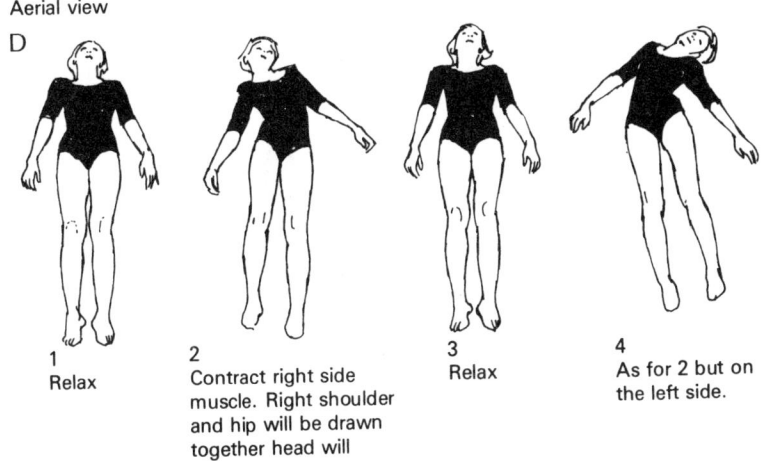

Aerial view

D

1 Relax

2 Contract right side muscle. Right shoulder and hip will be drawn together head will tilt slightly to left.

3 Relax

4 As for 2 but on the left side.

Teaching points

Imagine the muscles as a concertina that can be squeezed together (contracting) or opened out (extension). The head should naturally tilt in the opposite direction but again, this will come with practice. Try to make sure that all other parts of the body are relaxed.

Chest

This will improve the posture and loosen muscles around the shoulders.

A

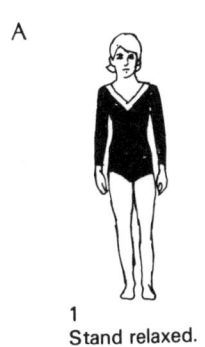

1 Stand relaxed.

2 Move arms behind and clasp hands straighten arms.

3 Gently bend head backwards taking rest of the body from waist upwards backwards also. Keep arms out.

4
Bring clasped hands and arms up over back and bend forwards from waist as far as possible. Hold.

5
Slowly straighten unclasp hands. Relax.

Teaching points

Count 5 for each movement. Do not strain.

B

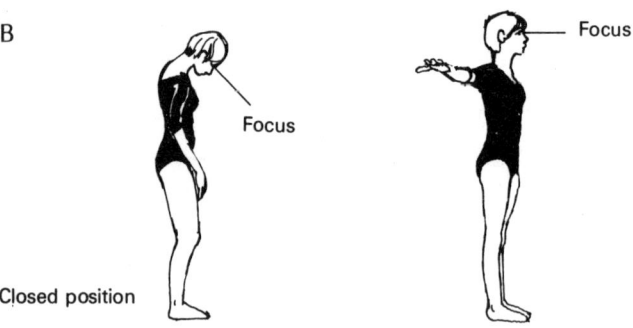

Closed position

1
Relax shoulders. Arms forward spine relaxed. Knees slightly bent. Head dropped.

2
Open arms out to shoulder level palms facing upwards. Chest open. Head up looking forward.

Teaching points

Position 1 is not difficult to achieve – it is a very relaxed position and the shoulder, hip and ankle joints should be in a straight line i.e. vertical. The tendency is for the children to lean forwards.

Spine

A

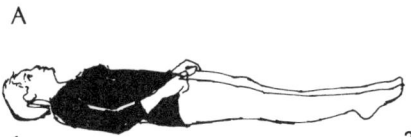

1
Relax lying on back on floor.

2
Slowly "peel" top half of body off the floor begining with the head.

3
Uncurl the spine slowly.

4
Sit straight lifting from base of spine.

From 4 go backwards to 3 2 1 and then repeat three times.

Teaching points

Try to lift each vertebra off the floor separately.

B

1
Sitting with a straight back.

2
Arch back head back.

3
Swing lower head to floor.

4
Try to let head touch floor first.

5
Relax.

6
Arch back

7
Push back to sitting position arching back, head back.

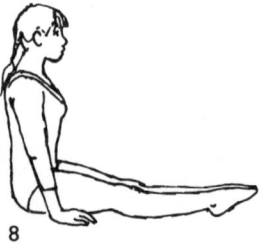

8
Back to sitting. Repeat twice

Teaching points

This is a difficult exercise and can be made easier if done in pairs. One child performs the exercise while the other gently holds the ankles of her partner. 1 - 5 is much easier than 6 - 8, so take care not to strain. The arms can help until all the class can do it on their own.

Hips

A

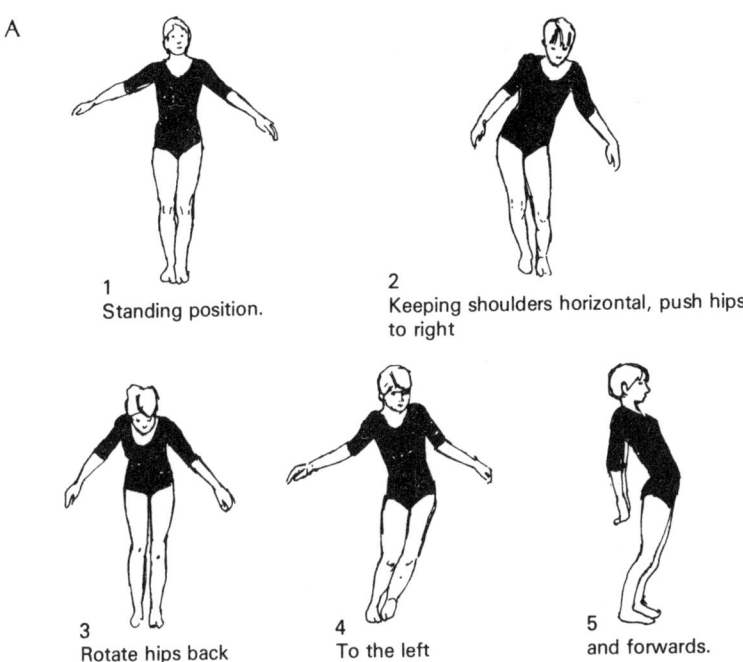

1 Standing position.
2 Keeping shoulders horizontal, push hips to right
3 Rotate hips back
4 To the left
5 and forwards.

Repeat in opposite direction

Teaching points
It is helpful to bend the knees when trying to rotate the hips.

B

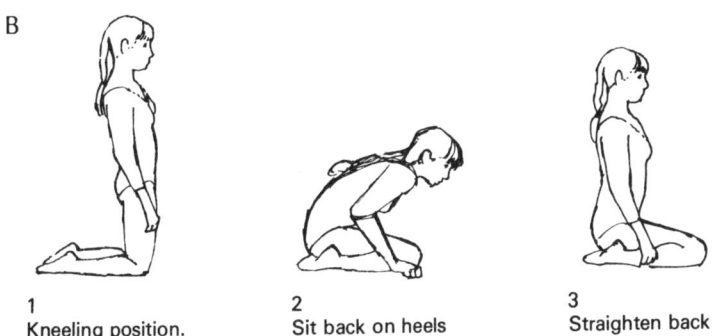

1 Kneeling position.
2 Sit back on heels
3 Straighten back

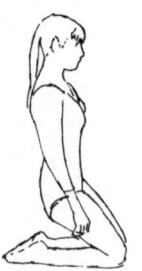 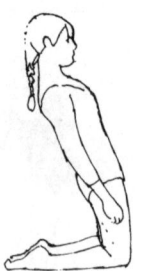  

4 Keeping shoulders still push hips up   **5** Body in alignment   **6** Lift as a unit   **7** Back to kneeling.

Repeat twice

Teaching points

This is very hard work, particularly for the thighs. When in position 3 it is helpful to put the arms behind the back and hands on the floor in order to push the hips through to 4. The back should not be arched, but kept straight, as if a metal bolt has been placed through the head, neck, back and legs for position 5.

Legs and feet

A

1 Standing legs apart feet slightly out-turned arms out at shoulder height.

2 Keeping back straight slowly bend knees keeping heels on the floor.

Repeat five times

3 Push back to starting position.

Teaching points

Keep the chest open and really use the legs to push down to 2 and press back up to 3. This will strengthen the leg muscles, particularly the thighs.

B

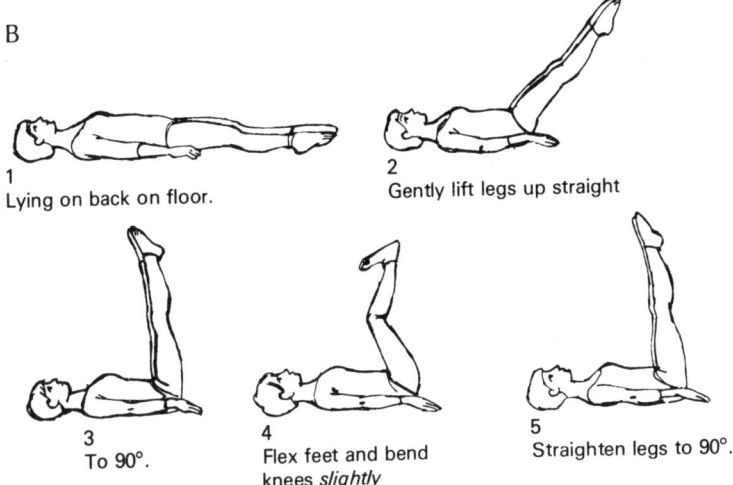

1 Lying on back on floor.
2 Gently lift legs up straight
3 To 90°.
4 Flex feet and bend knees *slightly*
5 Straighten legs to 90°.

Repeat five times. Gently lower legs from 5 down to floor.

Teaching points

This will stretch the calf muscles and ham strings. Lift legs to count of 8, hold for 4 counts, bend for 2, straighten for 2.

C

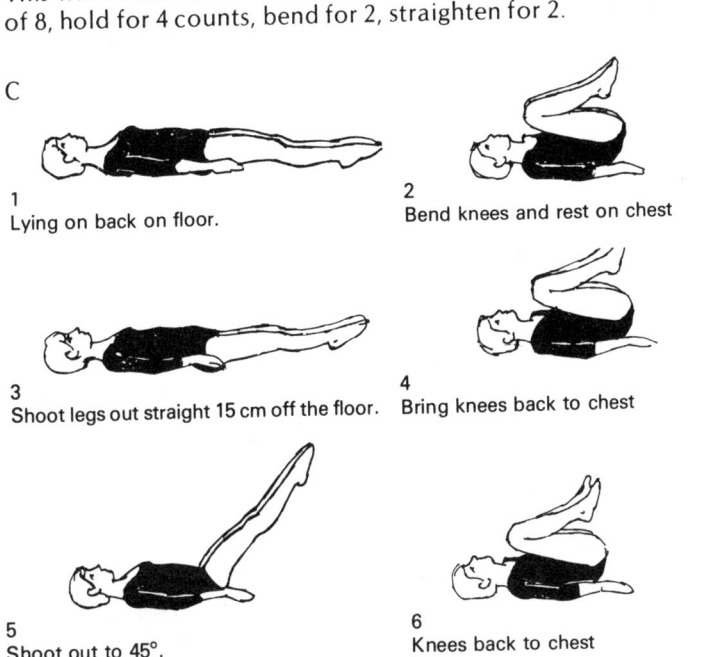

1 Lying on back on floor.
2 Bend knees and rest on chest
3 Shoot legs out straight 15 cm off the floor.
4 Bring knees back to chest
5 Shoot out to 45°.
6 Knees back to chest

7
Shoot legs up to 90°.
Repeat three times.

8
Lower legs straight *slowly* until back to starting position.

Teaching points

Keep hips on floor throughout. It is amazing how difficult it is to judge what is 6" from the floor when you cannot see your feet properly. It would help to get a partner to adjust legs to begin with. Try to get a simple rhythm going, e.g. bend for 2 counts, straighten for 2, bend for 2, straighten for 2, straighten to lower for 8 counts. This is also excellent for the tummy muscles.

D

1
Place hands flat on the floor. Sit on heels.

2
Straighten legs feet flat on floor

3
Release down to starting position. Repeat five times

Teaching points

It will be impossible for many to place the palms of their hands on the floor keeping their legs straight as in 2. To begin with, see that your class straighten their legs even if they cannot touch the floor with their fingertips. Gradually they will reach the floor. From position 2, see if your class can relax down to 3. If this is done properly, everyone should bounce naturally on their heels. This will stretch the ham strings.

E
1
Sitting position. Back straight legs out straight and apart. Point toes.

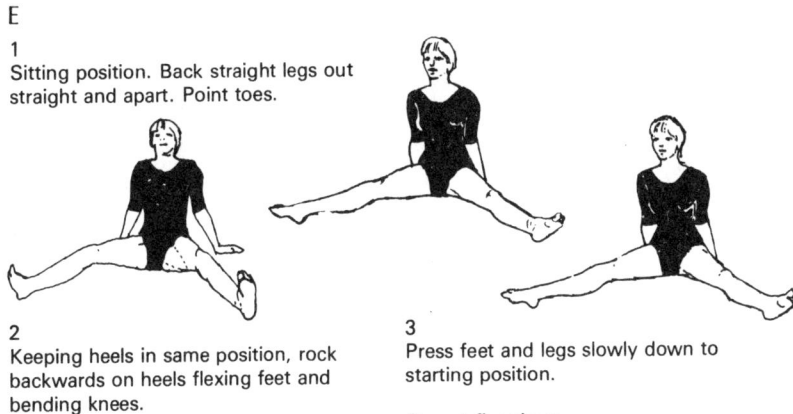

2
Keeping heels in same position, rock backwards on heels flexing feet and bending knees.

3
Press feet and legs slowly down to starting position.

Repeat five times

Teaching points

Point the toes as much as possible to ensure that the heels are in the correct position. Rock from front of heel to back so that the heels stay on the same spot. Lift sharply to 2 and press firmly to 3. Keep back upright but relax shoulders. Place arms behind on the floor with *light touch* to help keep the back straight, but do not lean heavily on them.

F

1
Sitting position. Back straight. Legs apart.

2
Try to get right *ear* towards right knee keeping right arm underneath ear! Lift left arm over left ear so that head is sandwiched in between. Point toes.

3
Lift back to centre

4
Repeat on left side.

Repeat three times on each side

Teaching points

Push for 2 counts stretching towards right foot for 2. Lift to 3 for 2 counts making sure that back returns to straight position, over to 4 for 2 counts, back to 1 and repeat. This may pull the ham strings (behind the knee) to begin with so be careful!

G

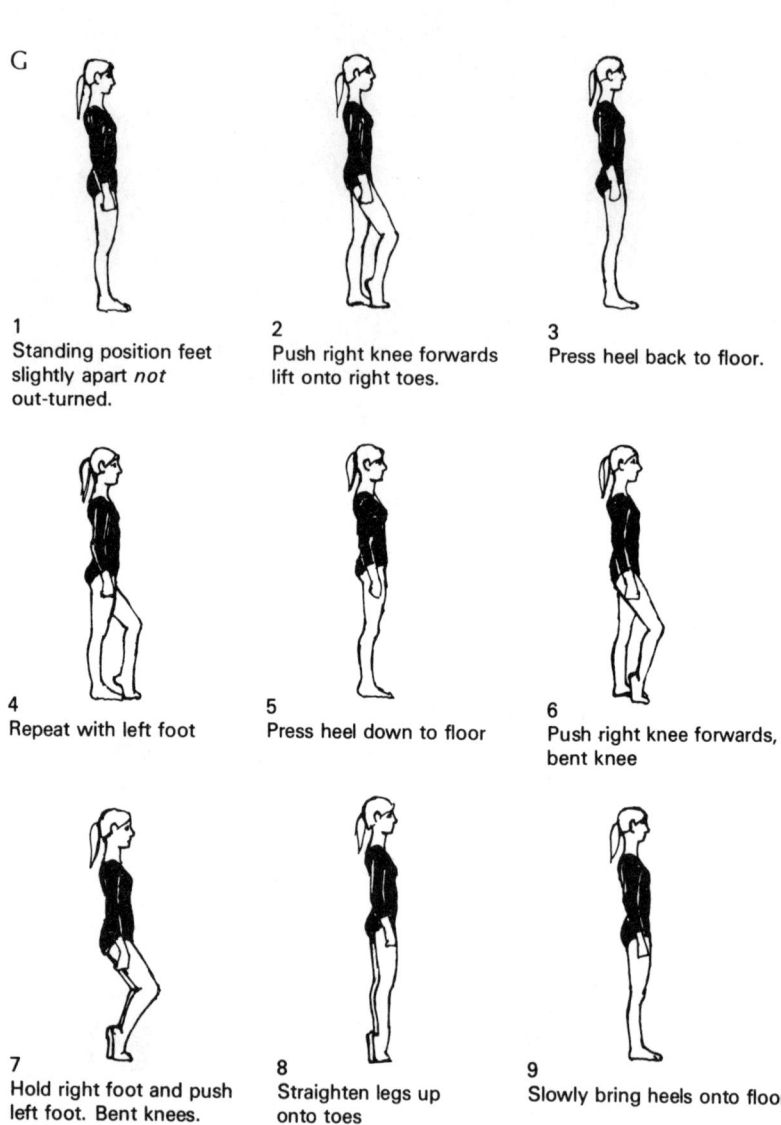

1 Standing position feet slightly apart *not* out-turned.

2 Push right knee forwards lift onto right toes.

3 Press heel back to floor.

4 Repeat with left foot

5 Press heel down to floor

6 Push right knee forwards, bent knee

7 Hold right foot and push left foot. Bent knees.

Repeat five times

8 Straighten legs up onto toes

9 Slowly bring heels onto floor.

Teaching points

Throughout keep the hips level, i.e. do not tilt when bending knees. Keep heels together when lifting in 8 and always ensure that feet are pushed forwards and not outwards which will create 'sickling' of the feet. Feel lightness when lifting to 8.

H

1 Sitting position. Bend left leg. Hold left instep with left hand. Keep back straight, right leg out towards diagonal.

2 Slowly try to straighten to count of 4. Keep back straight.

3 Left leg outwards. Hold for 4.

4 Lower left leg to count of 4.

5 Sitting position Hold for 4.

6 Change to right leg and repeat.

7

Teaching points

In 1 ensure left hand (arm) is inside knee i.e. in between legs. Support back with right hand as in diagrams. This exercise is strenuous and unless children are well warmed-up may pull the ham strings, so go gently.

Trunk

Flexibility is essential, but do not do too much if your class is not used to it. They will only be stiff and uncomfortable.

A

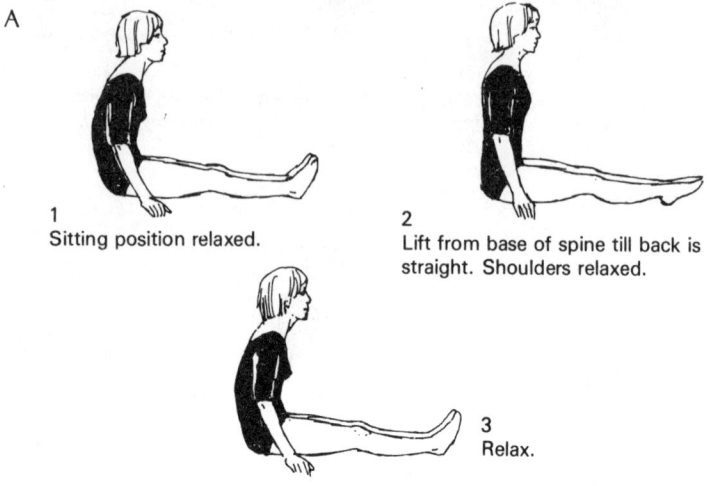

1
Sitting position relaxed.

2
Lift from base of spine till back is straight. Shoulders relaxed.

3
Relax.

Repeat five times

Teaching points

Introduce breathing rhythm to this. Breathe out for 1, in for 2, out for 3, repeat. Keep rhythm slow and even. Arms should be relaxed either side of body, fingertips touching the floor with a *light touch*.

B

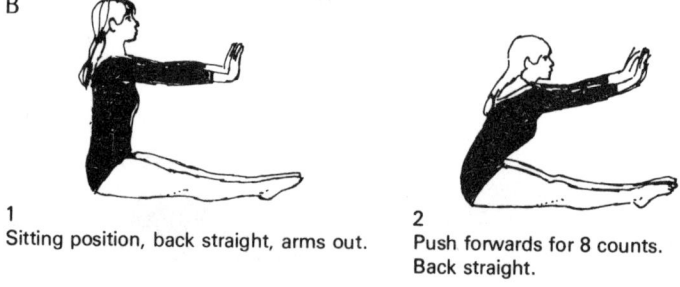

1
Sitting position, back straight, arms out.

2
Push forwards for 8 counts. Back straight.

3
Relax for 3 counts trying to put head onto knees.

Repeat twice

C

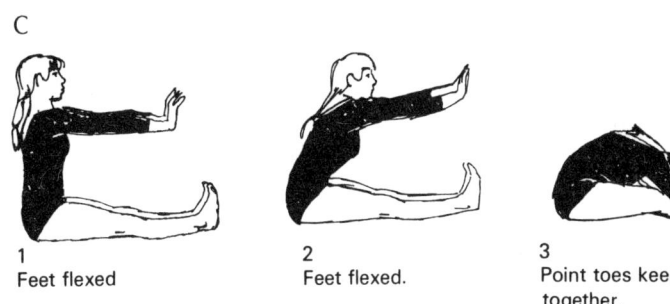

1
Feet flexed

2
Feet flexed.

3
Point toes keeping ankles together.

Teaching points

Ensure that back is straight for B C 1 and 2, shoulders relaxed. Imagine arms are pushing against a brick wall. For B C 3 do not expect all your class to be able to get their heads to their knees, and until they become more flexible make sure they do not strain themselves.

Excellent for attaining more mobility in back.

D

1
Place body in all fours position.

2
Curve spine towards ceiling, chin on chest.

3
Push spine towards floor head up.

Repeat 2 and 3 ten times

Teaching points

This should be done fairly quickly. Make sure the head is in the correct position in 2 and 3.

These can be done lying on the floor or standing, but the floor position is easier for beginners.

E

1
Lie on the floor, relax completely. Feet should turn-out. Hands should be facing upwards.

2
Try to push spine into floor. Head will go back slightly. Legs will bend slightly.

3
Relax.

Teaching points

This is fairly difficult as it involves trying to isolate individual muscles. 1 deals with the stomach muscles. Do not worry overmuch about the head position at first. This will get better with practice.

Complete actions

A

1
Standing tall, arms above head, shoulders relaxed.

2
Stretch right arm upwards focus up. Feel stretch down right side.

3
Stretch left arm up

4
Slowly lower arms down to sides.

Repeat six times.

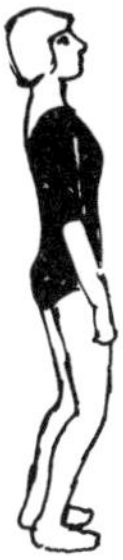

2 counts

2 counts

4 counts.

5
Relax half way position head will go back naturally, knees slightly bent.

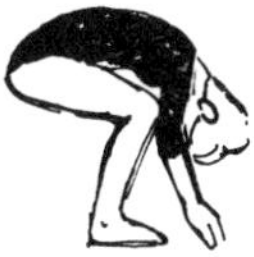

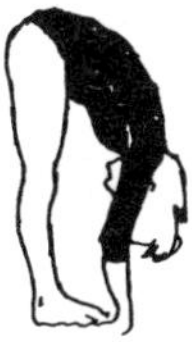

6
Let whole body go. Put hands down to stop falling.

7
Keep hands on floor if possible and straighten legs.

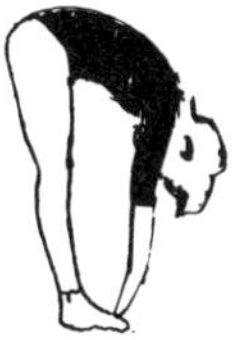

8
Slowly standing

4 counts

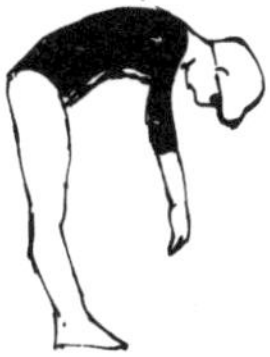

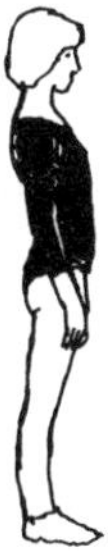

9
Slowly roll back up till standing.

Repeat twice

Teaching points

Note the counts and once class remembers each position introduce them and keep in time.

B

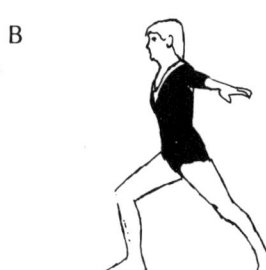

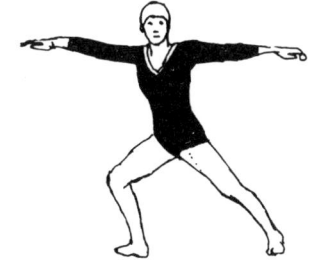

1
Place right leg forward, arms out at shoulder level. Hips and shoulders parallel to front of room. Bounce forwards 8 counts.

2
Keep hips parallel to front but twist head and shoulders to left. Bounce forwards 8 counts.

3
Lower to floor. Place hands either side of right let. Push left leg back further. Bounce up and down 8 counts. Hips facing floor.

4
Lift left arm up towards ceiling and bounce up and down 8 counts, hips facing floor.

Repeat with left leg in front.

Teaching points

Keep back leg straight throughout and make bent front leg do the work. Keep hips and shoulders facing in right direction. Excellent for strengthening leg muscles.

Space

Personal and general space

There are two ways of perceiving space; one is the area surrounding an individual known as the kinesphere or *personal space*. This area only extends as far as the body can reach. The *general space* normally refers to the whole area available to the dancer.

There is often a tendency for children to prefer to use only the personal space. This tends to limit the movement possibilities. In order for the general space to be used to the full, travelling needs to be emphasized. The teacher must therefore encourage the use of travel in order to add to the children's range. It is usually lack of confidence which causes the rather limited use of space and with perseverance and increasing familiarity it is easily overcome.

Levels

Within the personal space variation may be achieved by changing the level of the movement. Low level can be described as close to the floor or with different parts actually in contact with the floor. Medium level is between crouching and standing (i.e. between low and high). High level would involve elevation of the whole or part of the body, e.g. a jump or stretch upwards.

Movement is seldom done on one level alone so fluidity from one level to another should be practised and encouraged. Travelling using change of level would involve the use of the general rather than the personal space. This aspect of changing level is often neglected and can add variation to the expression.

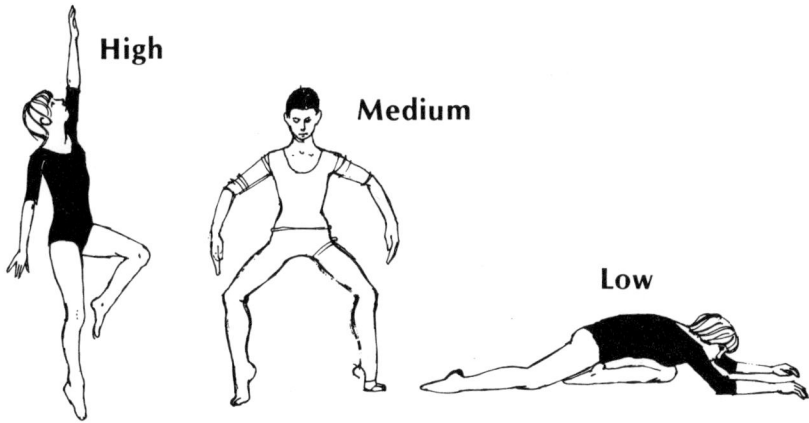

Dancing at a very low level often expresses fear; giving in to the security of the floor indicates uncertainty. Movement at a high level communicates a striving against the restraints of gravity (e.g. in classical ballet).

Directions

It is possible to move in many directions. The simplest of these are forwards and backwards. Sideways movement using both sides of the body is also elementary. Once these directions have been established then the upward-downward direction can be introduced. There are numerous angles between these directions that may be used effectively. For example, movement using the diagonal pathway has a very distinct, flowing quality of its own.

Rudolf Laban as a result of his own observations associated specific body actions with each direction. These can be of great help to the teacher or choreographer as they produce natural developments leading to very harmonious movement. They can also be changed around if disharmony is required. They are: travelling leading from forwards and backwards movement; opening and closing progressing into turning linked naturally with the sideways direction; rising and jumping from the upward direction; and sinking or falling from downward movement.

Peripheral and spoke-like movement

Movement can be initiated by or travel through the centre of the body. This can be described as spoke-like as it resembles the spokes of a wheel.

By avoiding the body centre, peripheral movement may be achieved. This leads to arch-like and often more continuous movement.

Combinations of both of these along with studies relating to other aspects of space may be studied in greater depth in Laban's book *Choreutics*.

Pattern

By combining and repeating different directions patterns are produced. These can be curved or straight, or combinations of both, and lead to many varying floor and air patterns.

It is often a useful exercise to concentrate on pattern as a starting place in the teaching of dance; partly because it is something concrete that can be easily observed by the teacher but mainly because it does not involve the children initially in feeling that they are exposing too much of themselves. Most children need to know the teacher and have confidence in her before they feel totally relaxed and involved, and pattern can be very expressive without the fear of showing emotion.

Here are some examples – straight curved, circular zig-zag, erratic

It maybe very difficult to recognise any clear shapes.

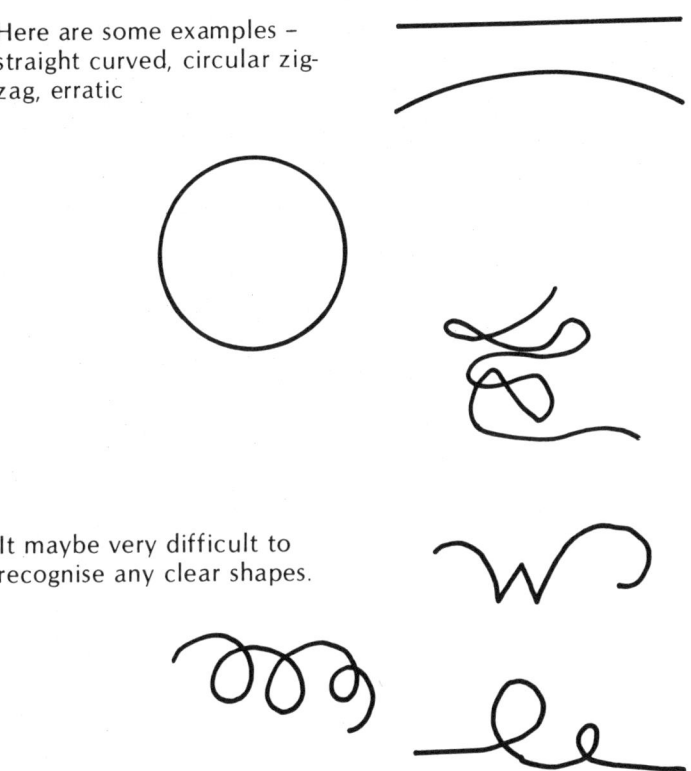

Quality-how the body can move and express

If the body is the instrument of the dancer we must not only consider what it can do and where it can move, but also the varying qualities necessary for expression. In his analysis of movement, Laban looks closely at the factors that dictate the dynamics of movement. We all have and develop our own particular characteristics. For example, our own way of walking shows individuality in speed, strength, size and flow. From this fundamental observation Laban formed his theories on Effort. He categorized them into the four elements of time, weight, space and flow.

The four elements

Time

This refers to the attitude of the dancer towards time. For example, lingering and indulging in time produces sustained or slow movement, as opposed to fighting or resisting the pressure of time, which leads to sudden or quick movement.

Weight

The response of the dancer to gravity creates an attitude towards weight. This manifests itself in giving in to or fighting against the force of gravity, producing either heavy or strong as opposed to light movement.

Space

This is often confusing as it again refers to the person's attitude towards the space rather than the areas in which the dancer can move. At the one extreme it leads to direct cutting movement and at the other indulgence and flexibility. The focus is indicative of the type of concentration, being either direct and penetrating or indirect and wide-ranging.

Flow

Flow is perhaps the most difficult quality to understand but possibly the easiest to observe, as it is so closely associated with communication. For example, in a conversation a person wishing to express a point of view will make full use of continouous free flow whereas a person in an uneasy situation may become withdrawn, abrupt and show clearly a bound or tight flow in their speech and gesture. The difference between extreme free flow and bound flow then becomes fairly obvious, the one being more abandoned and giving and the other showing restraint and control.

Combinations of Efforts

The elements are more often used in combination than in total isolation. Harmonious combinations can only be produced through the use of free flow, as in the structuring of a simple sentence. Bound flow leads to disjointed or inappropriately related movement. If the aim of the dance is to achieve grotesque movement, for example, then bound flow is the ingredient required.

Whilst looking at the extremes it must be remembered that there are degrees of each element. The complete mastery of movement is

dependent upon the acquisition of the total range of elements and also the range within each one.
Through observation Laban associated certain qualities of movement with specific personality traits. He spent a long time researching into the various patterns and rhythms within individuals and the known link between the body and mind became the basis for his findings and development of Effort notation.
Teachers may find through a more detailed study of Laban's work that they have a clearer understanding of individual personality as well as a deeper knowledge of dance as an expressive art.
Most people tend to favour one or two elements or extremes of elements. Obviously our aim is to develop as wide a range as possible in order to have the maximum possibilities for expression. This may also have ramifications in the development of the personality as the mind and body are so closely interrelated. If the mind and moods are seen through the body, it is possible that the movements of the body may have some effect on the mind, for example, in relaxation as practised in yoga.
Development along these lines in recent years has led to the use of many of Laban's ideas in the study of movement therapy in the diagnosing of illness and the curing of imbalances.

Stimuli

Dance is not purely functional in its movement and so the dancer needs inspiration in the form of a stimulus to achieve the expressive quality. A stimulus can be defined as 'a rousing influence or something that evokes activity'.
There are many different types of stimuli appealing to different senses. Generally in teaching, seeing and hearing are more commonly used. However, dance relies heavily upon both a kinesthetic and a tactile awareness. This is often the reason why many children are able to understand and express through movement more clearly than through the use of words.

Stimuli through sound

These include music, both recorded and live, of infinite variety. So closely linked is music with dance that it necessitates a section of its own. There are however many other types of sound which create stimuli for dance. Professionally-recorded sound-effects of almost anything can be obtained fairly easily. It is also possible to record one's own sounds as required. In some ways this is much more satisfactory, as the immediate requirements can be met exactly.

Also great satisfaction can be gained from actually finding and recording the different sounds.

Words are yet another important stimuli for dance – words on their own, for their sound or their meaning. Sometimes they may even combine the two. Poems, phrases, stories, plays, all inspire thoughts and expression. They can also be used as accompaniment by the dancers themselves as they move, or may be spoken, sung or recited by someone else.

The danger in using words is that they are in their own right so expressive that the dance often becomes secondary to or an exact interpretation of them. In most cases this is detrimental as it does not allow dance to use its own particular type of expression to the full.

Visual stimuli

The mind can be stimulated into action by sounds; it can also be similarly affected by light patterns, paintings, objects both natural and man-made. These can be created by the children as well as taken from more recognized sources. Patterns and paintings can be made and then interpreted or expressed again in movement. The same problems can arise as those mentioned with poetry or prose. With understanding and experience the essence of the material can be picked out and so the task becomes less confusing.

Lighting, although an aspect of visual stimuli, is very often connected solely with theatrical effects. Everyone knows how different natural light can affect the mood, the sunlight and the dullness change one's movement. Artificial lighting can be used not only to add mood to a dance but as an inspiration. This type of expression is limited to the facilities available but with the increase in the provision for lighting the possibilities should certainly not be ignored.

Kinesthetic awareness

The movement itself is so rich in possibilities that it can be its own stimulus. The enjoyment derived from moving and creating simple or complex combinations is satisfying. Having already discussed the ways in which the body can move, and the possibilities of kinesthetic awareness, the teacher must select or limit the relevant areas. This not only gives the stimulus but also increases the child's own vocabulary by encouraging a wider range of movement. In developing this range the opportunities for expression are greater.

Relationships as a stimulus

Dancing on one's own is a wonderful experience; it's like singing in the bath. It feels good and no one can tell you it looks otherwise.

Dancing on one's own in a room full of people can be a humiliating experience. Not only is concentration often difficult but the inhibitions are increased as the fear of making a fool of oneself becomes a very real threat.

For very young children dancing on one's own is often the only way. As soon as possible, however, children should learn to dance with others in twos or threes or small groups because for most people this is often where the most enjoyment can be found. The sharing of ideas, the experimenting, the communication of thoughts without words, the excitement of being in time, of moving with another is so stimulating.

Two people can dance together in different ways:

1 with each other, performing identical movements in identical time, producing a feeling of unity and harmony
2 with each other, performing the same movement at different times
3 with each other, performing different movement with the same phrasing
4 dancing together, quite separately, with a unity maintained by contact in some way, often just eye-contact
5 together, producing aggression or conflict by fighting movements, by action-reaction.

In threes the possibilities are similar but with an additional person the combination may be more complex. As a stimulus, two versus one can be very challenging dramatically as well as aesthetically.

Fours and fives are timeless combinations and as such require more experience or maturity in organization.

Larger groups are also stimulating to work with, as the flow of shape and movement through a group is an exciting experience, just as the face of a group working on an identical piece in time together gives a very powerful feeling as well as effect.

4 THE PREPARATION AND PRESENTATION OF DANCE

Preparation

Dance for many can be a natural expression, e.g. jumping for joy, or stamping in anger. It is, therefore, the teacher's task to guide these feelings towards the correct channels by providing the necessary outlets for them. The teacher is responsible for the structuring and building of the dance and a great deal of groundwork has to be completed before the idea of a dance can be presented to a class.

This will vary with the age and experience of the children. The teacher must understand their needs and development before selecting the method of presenting the material for the dance.

When a teacher begins to prepare a lesson, the following points are essential and must be thoroughly investigated.

The overall aims of dance

These have already been discussed.

The immediate and personal aims of the teacher

Besides wanting the children to move straight away, every teacher's aims will vary. If there are no aims then the lesson is meaningless, so it is vital that these are thought out carefully.

The needs and ability of the children

The complete range of ability in the class must be taken into consideration, and the material chosen should allow success within this. Do the children need to be made to feel secure, or do they need to use certain types of movement to enlarge their vocabulary? Both of these needs demand a method of limiting or restricting the movement required to begin with.

Selection of material

The teacher must select the stimuli and begin to break down the ideas into short-term objectives. The composition of the dance should clearly, throughout, be in line with the aims so that the class know exactly where they stand. When teaching a new class, it is essential to find out the group's dance knowledge and their reaction to certain areas before embarking on a series of lessons. A few light-hearted and varied lessons could show the teacher all she needed to know.

Composition

The theme or topic

This, for example, may be taken from a life situation such as war and peace, or from a movement idea such as changing levels or the use of strong and light movement. There must be an idea as a starting point and guideline for the class, but they too can find their own themes once they know the expectations of the teacher and how they can put their ideas into practice.

Material for the 'motif' based on the stimuli

What is a dance motif? A motif gives a basic premise on which to commence a dance. It is a brief sentence or phrase of movement, endeavouring to express something upon which children can develop and expand the theme or topic set before them. Motifs can be built up from a selection of the material mentioned earlier including body, space and effort. The motif should be clearly defined with a starting and finishing position. Establishing a good motif is the foundation of a sound and interesting dance.

Building of the motif

Once a motif is found, it can be developed. There are many ways of doing this:

1 It can be repeated in exactly the same way.
2 It can be increased in size.
3 The weight and time aspects can be changed.
4 It can be altered spatially – made larger, smaller, used at different levels, areas, directions or danced with a different attitude to the space.
5 There can be a change in flow.
6 It can be shortened or lengthened.
7 Different body parts may be used to express the original idea.
8 Emphasis can be placed at a different stage of the motif thereby altering the climax. The climax of the motif is very important as it can dictate the mood of the dance.

Motifs are made from a selection of these points but not all have to be used. If the class is working in small groups then motifs can be used in canon, shadowed and used at different levels. There are endless variations to be explored.

Structure of the dance

First of all, this will depend on the theme motifs and their development. We can break down the structure by a series of simple questions:

1 How many motifs are there to be? Usually a dance will contain several, but too many in the one dance can result in a disjointed, muddled effect, so it is better to use only a few and develop them to the full.
2 When, if at all, are they to be repeated?
3 How will they be combined and developed?
4 What will be the climax of the dance be? There may be several, or the dance may lead up to a dramatic climax and end suddenly.
5 How does the class link one movement to another? The *transition* from one movement to another is always difficult for children when they begin to learn dance, and time should be spent experimenting and exploring all the possibilities. These include jumping, rolling, sliding, stepping, spinning, turning and twisting.

The class should be told how much they are creating for themselves, and how much they can take from the teacher. They must also know what they can add or change, where they can travel, what length the dance must be and the precise expectations and limitations set by the teacher.

Composition of the lesson

When planning a dance lesson the following points have to be taken into consideration.

Selection of material

Obviously this will vary according to the age and ability of the children.

The teacher giving all the movement

Sometimes it may be necessary for the teacher to establish a particular type of movement; the class would then imitate a phrase or sequence taught by the teacher.

Part of the movement given

The stimuli, which may take many forms e.g. sculpture, hoops, ropes or poetry etc. may be given to particular qualities of the movement and the class left to respond accordingly.

All the movement created by the class

A movement idea may be presented to the class for them to experiment with. The role of the teacher here is to give clear limits within which the class should work, but all the work is done by the children with the teacher acting as a guide.

Final result

A dance may take up a long period of time or simply one lesson. If the dance takes up a long period of time then the series of lessons leading up to completion must be kept lively and interesting. Some groups will finish before others so they must be kept occupied and encouraged to develop their ideas to the full.

An example of a lesson

This is not the only way to plan and write down a lesson and each teacher will develop her own method as she becomes more experienced.

Theme   Body awareness with particular emphasis on leading a movement with different parts of the body.
Age of class   Middle school or first-year secondary (9–11 years).

MATERIAL	TASK AND HOW TO PRESENT MATERIAL
Warm-up	
1 Technique Select a swinging action from the technique section to loosen the whole body.	Face the class and mirror the movements. Demonstrate *slowly* a few times. Repeat with the children if necessary.
2 Trunk Simple curling and uncurling of the spine.	Get class to lie on the floor, feet facing the front. Slowly roll up to sitting position, and slowly lower back to floor. Remember head lifts off floor first and each vertebra folds separately off the floor.

Main lesson stimulus
1 Elastic
A simple but effective idea which helps central movement.

Warn the children a few weeks before the lesson, so that they can bring in their own elastic. Any colour will do, approximately 2½ cms wide as this will not cut into the skin. The class will be intrigued and will want to know what it is for!

2 How to use elastic

Attach elastic to one wrist and opposite ankle, e.g. right wrist and left ankle. Begin by making the children stay on the spot using their own *personal* space and let them experiment with the elastic. Encourage twisting, turning, stretching, getting into a tangle. What happens if they stretch the arm that has the elastic attached to it? How does it affect the opposite leg? Allow time to develop.

3 Adding other body parts

Take one step further:- Add other parts of the body, e.g. push elastic in any direction with free arm or leg. Begin to introduce change of levels, travelling into the *general* space, balance and off-balance. Allow time to develop.

4 Building up a phrase or sequence

By now the class will have had time to experiment, so encourage them to select certain movements they like and put them together to form a phrase or sequence. Remember to tell the class to repeat the sequence until they know it. Give a set time to finish.

5 The finished phrase	Show half the class at a time. Begin by each child taking up a starting position. Tell the class when to start, and when they have finished to hold still for a short time and repeat their phrase. Let the remaining half of the class sit, watch and observe unusual movements and try to notice why they are different. Show the other half of the class in the same manner.
Calming down Before the class is dismissed, they should have a period of time to unwind and collect themselves together before going to their next lesson.	Remember to leave enough time for the class to change. In a space facing the front, stretch upwards slowly and then relax. Roll back up to standing.
Dismiss class to changing rooms.	

Development

Repeat phrases through quickly the following week. Then take same phrases and repeat it exactly *without* the elastic. The children will find they need far more control. This idea can be developed even further by attaching the elastic to different parts of the body, or even working in pairs and attaching one end of the elastic to one child and the other to the partner.

Presentation

In trying to help the teacher present the material involved in a dance lesson, there are many different aspects to consider. The dance teacher needs all the qualities of a good teacher and more!
 The advantage of dance can also be a disadvantage for the teacher, for there are no rules as such. There is no right or wrong way to dance so the teacher is responsible for setting her own aims

and standards. This is a real challenge, particularly for the inexperienced teacher.

As with any activity in which children are free to move about, organization is vital and the structure of the lesson or learning situation is as important as the structure of the dance itself. Once children are familiar with the discipline, the individual needs can be more easily catered for. It is the very exceptional child who is not reliant upon the teacher for motivation or inspiration in some way. Therefore an understanding of the children and adequate preparation are essential ingredients for successful presentation. A number of other important factors are listed below.

Setting the scene

If music is to be used, it is very important to familiarize the children with it, even if just by playing it when they arrive in the room. If music is not used then perhaps the stimuli, whatever it might be, could be presented in a similar fashion. Some useful methods of beginning dance can be through a purely technical approach or starting children on national or folk dancing, or even leading them from the kind of dance they may be used to doing at discotheques or youth clubs. This will depend entirely on the teacher and, of course, the age and knowledge of the children. Whatever the method used, they can gradually be weaned away from one type of dance and given or shown opportunities to add new qualities and dimensions to their movements.

Teaching through doing

Talking about dance may have its place at times, but 'doing' is essential. Initial warm-up or technique is a time to include relevant vocabulary for the topic in hand. For example, in a lesson where the dance is energetic and aggressive, the warm-up should include this type of movement.

Each week, at least one new movement should be added to the repertoire. Gradually, different areas can be stressed and it will be found that children will automatically draw from previous experience. So long as the whole programme is carefully planned, the vocabulary that they acquire for communication through dance should increase week by week.

Presentation of stimuli

Usually this follows the warm-up and the teacher must ensure that every child is aware of the stimulus so that various responses can be made.

Improvisation and selection

The stimulus may be given to the children and the teacher may select a motif from their improvisation. On the other hand, the teacher may let the children improvise and select for themselves. With either method, the teacher must guide the class in the right direction. This can be done by asking questions such as: How do you want to move from A to B and what parts of the body will you use? Gradually as the dance progresses, formations will arise with this helpful guidance.

Building up from the teacher's direct motifs

The class may be given a motif by the teacher and asked to develop it. Here again, the teacher must direct them along the right path.

Experimentation and limitation of movement ideas

Clear limits must be set within which the class is to work, otherwise nothing may be gained. The teacher must be ready to cope with many problems and children should be encouraged to perform simple movements until their vocabulary increases. Children enjoy exploring and discovering different movements and it is vital that they experiment and find out exactly what they can do with their bodies. It is here that the teacher must provide the opportunity for pupils to realize the capacities of their own bodies.

It depends upon the age and experience of the children as well as the subject matter as to which of these methods is the most useful. Very often a combination of them all is possible.

The teacher's role

Once the basic factors have been established the teacher should be prepared both mentally and physically. The following points are often overlooked and although they may appear obvious, they may be of assistance and are certainly valid when presenting dance to a class.

Positioning of the teacher

When confronted with a class, the positioning of the teacher is important. There is no hard and fast rule as to exactly where one should stand, and each individual will differ according to which aspect of dance they are teaching. For example, when teaching technique, the teacher should face the class and remember to mirror the movements that are being performed, otherwise children will get very confused by the right and left side of the body. Once the class are familiar with certain technique movements, the teacher can move around the class to correct any faults.

No matter what type of dance or topic is being taught, children should be able to see and hear the teacher at any given time. This will not only help attain discipline but also build up a sense of security. If music is being used, then the equipment should be close at hand. Nothing is more annoying than having to rush to the opposite end of the room or up onto a stage to stop and start a recording.

Correct use of voice and words

Do not expect children to understand dance 'jargon'. It is quite easy to find simple terms to describe complex statements. At the same time, the voice should be clear and lively expressing the mood required. Speak when necessary but not continuously. The children are there to learn to dance and not to listen to your voice.

Dress and use of equipment

Each individual should strive to attain self-discipline. We cannot teach this but we can certainly help children to acquire it by how we act ourselves. Consequently, appearance is of great importance in a lesson. The correct attire is a prerequisite; girls should be encouraged to wear leotards and boys to wear vest and shorts. This will mean that movement is not restricted and it makes the teacher's task much easier. Footless tights can also be worn, but the feet should be kept bare for safety. A highly polished floor can be dangerous even if the task in hand is sliding! Some dances may require other types of dress but leotards can still form the basic uniform.

Before using music, find out what type of equipment is available and whether or not it is possible to use it in the dance area. Tape recorders are the most serviceable as they can be stopped and started at will and they are easier to use. Good recordings should be made and most schools now have excellent facilities which make this possible. During a lesson, the equipment should be within close reach of the teacher. If you are fortunate enough to be able to put on a dance performance for parents and friends, then make sure all your music is taped in sequence for your convenience. This helps significantly in the smooth running of a display.

Relationships

It is the teacher's role to make a class feel at ease, particularly a new class who may feel very apprehensive and inhibited. You too may be new and feel the same, but how you react will reflect upon the class, so be confident, firm yet amiable. The relationship which grows between the teacher and class is a valuable one and should be thought of as such. A good sense of humour is helpful and can create a comfortable and relaxed atmosphere, although the class should also remain controlled. For teachers just beginning their careers this may be hard at first, but once they know the children and learn their reactions to certain areas, a good solid relationship can be formed and particular problems that may arise can be dealt with more easily.

Size of groups

The organization of the class into the appropriate size of groups is another influential factor in successful teaching. If the children are very young then they tend to have more difficulty in adjusting to larger groups as well as working on their own. Probably twos, threes and fours are the most practical, and gradually as they get older and increase their movement experience they will learn to cope with larger numbers. These may have to be carefully thought out by the teacher. In the larger groups, one child nearly always becomes the leader and, whilst the others may contribute readily, they often need a spokesman. A group with no leader may achieve nothing just as a group with too many may end up arguing. If younger children are left to choose their own groups care must be taken that one child is not left out. The teacher must be able to deal with this situation should it arise, but better still, try not to let it happen in the first place.

Observe and help

Once the class have been given a task to perform, whether individually or in groups, the teacher must be able to observe carefully and give them help. Sometimes a class comment said aloud will help them become more aware of the task set and will continuallly give them new ideas. However, there are times when the teacher will have to move around the class watching small groups working on their own. Children enjoy this attention but the teacher must ensure that she spends her time equally among the groups. Encouragement and praise should be given often and not only will your classes want to improve their movement but they will enjoy doing it.

Demonstration and constructive criticism

There may be circumstances when the teacher needs to demonstrate a particular type of movement. This should be done well and repeated several times. There are other times when a group chosen by the teacher displays an action or a task set. It is important to point out how they have mastered the task so that the class themselves learn to observe each other's work. Each lesson may be a separate entity or contribute to the whole and culminate in a complete dance at the end of a series of lessons. It is important that there is a goal at the end for children to aim at. This is the perfect time for them to see each other's work and, at the end of each group performance, give constructive criticism. This means that the children can, for a while, enjoy taking over the teacher's role and help each other under careful guidance. Not only are they now learning to observe each other's movements but they are also building up their own vocabulary simply by watching their contemporaries.

The ultimate aim of a teacher in preparing and presenting a lesson to a class is to be able to adapt a scheme of work to the whole, so that the least and most able pupils can participate fully and obtain enjoyment and satisfaction from their dance lessons.

5 PRACTICAL EXAMPLES OF DANCE TOPICS

To add more depth and practical suggestions to the previous chapter we now include a list of topics with the suitable age range and the type of movement that could be used as a starting point for each topic. Any helpful hints on music or organization have also been included wherever possible.

Generally the topics for the younger age range will be less abstract in approach and result but could equally well be taken again with an older age range with a different teacher. For the older age range the movement suggestions are usually taken from the essence of the topic in hand, and this is where the clear insight and preparation of the teacher is important. For example, 'puppets' can be used with very young children in a simple way to help isolate body parts, and with a partner for observation of simple movement. With the more experienced dancer or the older age range some very exciting work can be created from the puppet idea; intricate movements; looking at the possibilities of how everyone is a puppet in the hands of society and fate, the strings being pulled by external forces such as fashion, values held by society etc; one's continuing struggle to pull one's own strings and what happens in marriage when they must be pulled in the same direction etc. Such work involves really looking into the problems of life as well as into the mastery of movement.

Idea	Age Range
Natural Forces Earthquakes Volcanoes Hurricanes/Storms Weather generally	Young Middle Older
Nature Trees Flowers Rocks Sea	Older – tends to become too mime-like with younger children.
Important Events in Life Birth Death Baptism	Older – rather abstract for young children.
Normal Everyday Life A day in the life of School Holidays Work Shopping Travelling	Any age
Stories Myths – Midas and the Golden Touch Biblical – Jonah and the Whale Historical – War Scientific – Space Fairy – Grimms, Andersen Drama – Contemporary or traditional Melodrama – as used in silent movies, etc.	Suitable for all ages. Short and simple for younger age. Could become longer and more involved for older ones.
Films, Shows	Any age but especially good for adolescents.

Movement Source	Helpful Hints
Efforts: time, weight, space, flow. Space: directions, levels, areas. Body action. Allow for great variety in mixture of learned motifs and improvisation.	Music very helpful. Lighting effects.
Space: particularly direct and flexible, aesthetic patterns, group formations.	Can produce beautiful images if carefully directed. Avoid *being* a flower or tree. Growing could be a subject on its own.
Could draw from any movement source but should be limited to the subject in hand, i.e. appropriate qualities.	Can produce very involved abstract and meaningful dances. Avoid portraying people wherever possible.
Occupations, mimes, comic. Repetition of simple motifs; note individuals or groups; enlarge movements. Maintain phrasing and rhythmical quality.	Can be people but actions should be exaggerated. Use of unusual parts of body and show action required. Story-line helpful to maintain discipline in the composition.
Again specific topics require individual selection but all generally dramatic, therefore Effort will play a large part.	Really get to the essence of the stories. Keep structure very clear. Use of change and repetition of motifs will make suitable links where necessary. Abstract as much as possible.
Use of the movements as seen in film or show, e.g. *Chorus Line* or *Saturday Night Fever*.	A very good lead-in for the less experienced – usually able to identify with this type of dance having seen more of it.

Idea	Age Range
Abstract Ideas Concepts Light v. dark War v. peace Life v. death Harmony v. discord Love v. hate	Most
Social Situations and Comments Drugs Alcohol Vandalism Violence	Older
Old age Adolescence Divorce Sports Recreations Children's Games	Mostly older, but Sports or Children's Games possibly could be adapted for younger age group.
Ritual Dance Rain dances African, Indian Red Indian Worshipping Funeral, Wedding (Roman, Greek or Old English style)	Any age – younger ones especially.
News Recent events Robbery Murder Disaster	Any age
Social Dancing Disco Ballroom Country	Any age

Movement Source	Helpful Hints
Contrasts in Effort, space and relationships, e.g. Light could be: free flowing, light, flexible, communicating. Dark could be: bound, strong, direct/flexible, isolated etc.	Useful as partner or group-work. Simple clear ideas easily translated with movement. A very useful starting place for more abstract dance.
Taken from close examination of idea and observation of movement involved.	Needs either very strong story-line or tight structure.
Look at the everyday actions involved and pick out the symbolic movements, adapting them to the required phrasing etc; but they should still have something instantly recognizable about them.	More complex subjects but offering a great range of possibilities.
Study the ethnic culture involved and movement ideas will become obvious.	Structure very clearly, with or without story-line. Costume useful to add authenticity.
Actions – occupations. Drama – similar to previous ideas on 'A day in the life of'. Group work.	Take from the story the important facts and rewrite in dance, emphasizing a few important ideas.
The set dances themselves or made-up steps in the style of the dance.	Very useful addition to children's vocabulary. Also important in social education and understanding the function of dance.

Idea	Age Range
Folk and National Dancing Greek Israeli Rumanian Hungarian German Scottish	Any age
Puppets	Young Adults Older
Machines	Young Middle Older
Fighting	Young Middle Older

Purely Movement Topics
The body actions – What is the body doing?
Relationships – With whom or what is the body relating?
Quality – How is the body moving?
Space – Where is the body moving?

Probably the most commonly used of all ideas for dance is the movement itself. In limiting the choice the range is increased. It can eventually lead into any one of the topics previously mentioned, either within the dance lesson or much later on, e.g. lifting, lowering, supporting with change of level. Could be danced in its own right or used as an introduction to a dance on friendship.

Movement Source	Helpful Hints
Usually body movement based on dances from other countries. Societies. Records. Observation. Creating own steps in the national style is also a possibility.	Again increases vocabulary and rhythmic awareness. Costume adds the characteristics of each country. Good as a lead-in to more creative dance.
Body actions: isolated body parts. Bound/free flow. Partner work – mirroring, shadowing, make-up simple motifs.	'Puppet on a string' – useful, simple repetitive tunes. Clarify all different types of puppets.
Body actions: isolated body parts. Bound flow, directions, levels. Contrasting time, action-reaction, develop from simple motif.	Sounds usually better than music. Percussion good. Identify machine parts and function.
Effort actions, e.g. punch, thrust, press etc. Change of size and speed levels, action-reaction. Different body parts. Contraction. Use of repetition.	Slow-motion useful. Enlarge movement space between strokes.
The movement itself from: body, effort, space, relationship.	Limit to one or two ideas only to begin with, then develop to possibly one from each section.

6 THE USE OF MUSIC

Music and dance are interrelated. Dance has always used music as a stimulus and for accompaniment, but dance is not totally dependent on music and can exist on its own.

Music as stimulus

In starting dance with children who have had little or no experience, music may play a vital role. The use of familiar music immediately creates a more relaxed atmosphere which helps inspire confidence. There are many popular recordings which are totally unsuitable for dance, but with careful selection it is possible to find some that are more than adequate. It may be possible with more experienced children actually to compose the music as the dance develops. This situation may prevent the dance from becoming dependent upon the structure of the music. However, prerecorded music can be edited and even superimposed with different rhythms, to create a less rigid form.

Music as accompaniment

With technique

The principle behind doing technique to music is that the music will keep the rhythm and help the movement to flow more easily.

It is important that the technique is appropriate to the music used. The phrasing and structure of the music, as well as the rhythm, must be allowed to influence the phrasing, structuring and rhythm of the exercises. To take a simple example, a tune which has a verse and a chorus can be used for two different exercises to alternate or to follow the structure of the music.

With a pianist

If you are fortunate enough to have a pianist for dance lessons, specific rhythms and phrasing can be made up as required. This is often difficult for the inexperienced teacher and it does require building up a very good understanding with the pianist. Both folk dance and technique are particularly suited to this type of accompaniment.

As a presence

Background music has its place in dance by highlighting or emphasizing particular sections of the dance. This can be done with matching, blending or contrasting types of music. For example, to set a slow dance against an incongruous musical background can emphasize the importance of the communication.

Percussion

With percussion children can add a dynamic quality to their already-composed movement. This can be improvised or prerecorded. Once the organizational problems of using percussion have been overcome the children can benefit considerably in rhythmical vocabulary.

The choice of music

The theme or topic generally influences the choice of the music. If music is to be used as an accompaniment, it is often more successful to choose more subdued pieces. When selecting the music for a particular theme there are many different aspects to consider.

1 The music should have something of the qualities that are to be emphasized in the dance, e.g. if elevation is important, the music should not be heavy and drawn-out. Both the teacher and the pupils should enjoy the music for its suitability even if not as a piece on its own.
2 Remember that in well-balanced dance there should be moments of contrast, however brief, and if the music is too dance-like or repetitive it is difficult to attain enough variation.
3 A dance can be any length but once the statement has been made too much repetition may destroy the expression.
4 A full orchestral symphony would be unsuitable for a solo as it would tend to smother the dance. On the other hand a large-group dance needs a more complex piece of music to balance the composition.

It is also possible to draw from the chosen music a suitable theme, particularly if the movement itself is the stimulus. If the teacher is giving the topic to the children, the theme should be related in some ways to the music in order to prevent complications. It might be possible to work on more obscure ideas with smaller groups or if the children choose the themes themselves.

Composing to music

Having selected an appropriate piece of music it is necessary to discover its timing and structure. It is helpful to have a basic knowledge of music in order to pick out the different forms. In popular music there is often a simple verse-chorus structure known as A B form. Here there need only be two different motifs, A and B, which can then be developed. Variations on this can be numerous, for example, with an introduction and conclusion you could have A, B, C, BC, D. This type of music is probably most suitable for technique as it is very repetitive. Other forms can be broken down in a similar way if a letter is allocated for each new section, e.g. A, B, A, CDBA, EFBA etc. Every time the music is repeated it is given the same letter. Exactly the same system can be applied to the most complicated of classical compositions. It may take longer to pick out the sections as they could be more heavily disguised.

If the music is complicated it is possible, instead of creating a motif for each new section, to use the more obvious A B sections as the focal points. The dance can then be developed across the difficult parts with developments of the original motifs.

Here is an example from the beginning of Andrew Lloyd-Webber's *Variations* taking the Introduction and Theme from Paganini's *Caprice in A Minor*. We have given each theme a letter and each variation a number:

$$A\ B\ B$$
$$A\ B\ B$$
$$A_1\ B_1\ (A_2\ A_2\ B_2\ B_2)$$
$$C(A)\ C(B)$$
$$A_3\ B_3\ B_3\ A_4\ B_4$$

The technical problems of using music

The choice of equipment is important. For everyday use a cassette player is all that is necessary as long as the quality is good and the volume is sufficient for the size of the room. A record player may be used but damage to the records can easily occur. A combination of tape cassette and record player in a music centre is ideal so that recording can be simple.

For special editing it may be better to use a reel-to-reel tape recorder, as it offers possibilities of double-tracking and cutting.

Building up a collection of suitable music is helpful, especially if the teacher categorizes the music under the relevant headings, i.e. what is suitable for technique or for a particular quality of movement.

Generally speaking the more expensive the equipment the better the result, but it is possible to make do with simple, less costly equipment when necessary.

CONCLUSION

In writing this book we have tried to show that dance is a natural form of expression with no stereotyped rules and regulations. The teacher of dance should not feel inhibited by her own lack of technical knowledge in any one style of dance. The ability to draw from the children the desire to dance by understanding their needs is far more important. We hope that the guidelines we have set out here will help the teacher to understand the needs of the children, their capabilities and limitations, and so make better use of the available material.

Dance is a very demanding subject to teach, for not only has the teacher to be constantly thinking of new ideas, but the approach chosen will depend upon her relationship with and understanding of each group. This relationship is especially important in dance because of the dependence of the class on the teacher. As we mentioned earlier, rules can only be made to fit the situation as it arises and the teacher must be responsible for establishing her own methods.

In giving examples of topics and a sample of a lesson plan we hope that we have gone some way to help the teacher to feel a little more secure. Having been successful through good organization and using appropriate material, the teacher should feel confident enough to pursue a more individual approach.

Communication can occur in many ways but the basic skill stems from understanding and empathy. Because in dance it is the body that communicates, understanding must come through a knowledge of the implications of movement. Our aim should be to avoid the nebulous, formless, hesitant shapes that are so often simply self-indulgent. Each movement should be chosen to express a precise meaning rather than just the feeling of the dancer. As Doris Humphreys says: 'It is often difficult for the student to let himself go and cross over from the lifetime restraints of socio-religious habits, to those of unregenerate man that are often demanded by dramatic ideas. He may be able to feel these things; but having always restrained himself from expressing them, he does not know the vocabulary for them.'

We hope that by providing the teacher with some vocabulary in the technique section and some insight into the analysis of movement in the section on making a dance, that dance in schools may become a more expressive art form as well as a healthy recreational activity.

BIBLIOGRAPHY

BEST, D. (1978) *Philosophy and Human Movement* Hemel Hempstead: Allen and Unwin
DOUBLER, M.H. (1957/1972) *Dance: A Creative Art Experience* Washington: Wisconsin Press
FORSTER, R. (1976) *Knowing in My Bones* London: A. & C. Black
HUMPHREY, D. (1959) *The Art of Making Dances* New York: Grove Press Inc.
LABAN, R. (1948) *Modern Educational Dance* London: Macdonald & Evans
LABAN, R. (1963) *Modern Educational Dance* (2nd edition revised L. Ullmann) Plymouth: Macdonald & Evans
LABAN, R. (1966) *Choreutics* (Ed. L. Ullmann) Plymouth: Macdonald & Evans
LANGER, S.K. (1953) *Feeling and Form* London: Routledge & Kegan Paul
MCKITTRICK, D. (1972) *Dance* Basingstoke: Macmillan
NORTH, M. (1973) *Movement Education* London: Temple Smith
NORTH, M. (1972) *Personality Assessment through Movement* Plymouth: Macdonald & Evans
PRESTON-DUNLOP, V. (1963) *A Handbook for Modern Educational Dance* Plymouth: Macdonald & Evans
RUSSELL, J. (1965) *Creative Dance in the Primary School* Plymouth: Macdonald & Evans
RUSSELL, J. (1969) *Creative Dance in the Secondary School* Plymouth: Macdonald & Evans
SMITH, J. (1976) *Dance Composition* London: Lepus Books